P9-DHC-632

26

POLITICAL UNTOUCHABLES
The Tories and the '45

Political Untouchables

The Tories and the '45

Eveline Cruickshanks

Duckworth

First published in 1979 by
Gerald Duckworth & Co. Ltd.
The Old Piano Factory
43 Gloucester Crescent, London NW1

© 1979 by Eveline Cruickshanks

All rights reserved. No part of this
publication may be reproduced, stored in a
retrieval system, or transmitted, in any
form or by any means, electronic, mechanical,
photocopying, recording or otherwise, without
the prior permission of the copyright owner

ISBN 0 7156 1334 0

Printed in Great Britain by
Ebenezer Baylis and Son Ltd.
The Trinity Press, Worcester, and London

Preface

The story of the '45 in Scotland has been told so often that the late Sir James Fergusson suggested there ought to be a law to prevent any more books on the subject. Yet these works have largely ignored the European context out of which the '45 arose and in which alone it could succeed. Historians on this side of the Channel have assumed that for the French the rebellion was a useful 'diversion' from the war in Flanders, without taking any systematic look at French sources. French historians, who knew that Louis XV was in earnest in seeking to restore the Stuarts, did not appreciate that conditions in eighteenth-century England made open expression of Jacobitism impossible. Being part English, part Scottish, and part French, I may have an excuse for an undertaking which will most probably arouse the ire of historians of all three nations. At any rate, alternate education in England and in France has convinced me that European history seen in purely national terms will not do.

I am grateful for permission to use the manuscripts of Her Majesty the Queen, of the Duke of Beaufort, the Duke of Bedford, the Duke of Devonshire and the trustees of the Chatsworth Settlement, the Duke of Northumberland, the Earl of Harrowby, the Treasurer and Masters of the Bench of Lincoln's Inn, and in France those of M. Martial de la Fournière of the Quai d'Orsay, M. le Général Guinard of the service historique du Ministère de la Défense Nationale, and M. le Contre-Amiral Fliche of the service historique de la Marine.

I am indebted to Professor Ian Christie for making a number of suggestions on the contents of this book, to John Brooke and Howard Erskine-Hill for useful discussions on some points made, to John Kerslake of the National Portrait Gallery for advice on illustrations, and to Peter Hasler of the History of Parliament Trust for reading the final draft. Dr Linda Colley has kindly allowed me to read her thesis on the Tory party from 1727 to 1760, and I have benefited from several exchanges with her. My greatest debt is to the late Romney Sedgwick, a staunch Whig, whose wit and erudition I greatly admired, for a series of discussions, heated at times, but, as I well know, much enjoyed on both sides.

E.C.

Contents

Illustrations

'On the Abjuration'

Our fathers took oaths as we take our wives
For better for worse, and kept them their lives,
But we take the oaths like whores, for our ease,
We whore and rogue, and part when we please

(anonymous poem in the manuscripts of the
Duke of Beaufort at Badminton)

Abbreviations

Add.	Additional manuscripts in the British Library.
AECP Ang.	Archives étrangères, correspondance politique, Angleterre at the Quai d'Orsay.
AEM & D. Ang.	Archives étrangères, mémoires et documents, Angleterre.
CJ	*Journals of the House of Commons.*
Guerre	Manuscrits du departement des forces terrestres at the château de Vincennes.
H. Walpole Corresp.	*The Correspondence of Horace Walpole,* Yale ed.
HC	*History of Parliament, The House of Commons 1715–1754*; ed. Romney Sedgwick.
HMC	*Historical Manuscripts Commission reports.*
Marine	Manuscrits du departement de la marine, in the Archives Nationales, Paris.
Parl. Hist.	Cobbett's *Parliamentary History.*
SP	State Papers in the Public Record Office, London.
VCH	*Victoria County History.*

All the dates in England are given in the Old Style with the year beginning on 1 January. Documents written on the Continent are given in both Old and New Style.

Quotes in foreign languages have been translated.

1

The Tories and the Party System

Politics in the reigns of the first two Georges (1715–1760) have usually been looked at from the point of view of the reign of George III (1760–1820), which is viewing them through a distorting mirror. Political thinking was still dominated by the great events of the Revolution of 1688 and the Restoration of 1660, much as ours still is by those of the Second and First World Wars. In dealing with the eighteenth century, and with the Tory party in particular, historians have often been guilty of hindsight and of knowing consistently better than contemporaries.

Traditionally the Tories stood for the support of the Crown and the Anglican Church, and for hatred of a standing army which they equated with the rule of Oliver Cromwell. Basking in the sun of royal favour under Charles II and in the early years of James II's reign, they had enjoyed a monopoly of office to the exclusion of the dissenters and Roman Catholics. They showed little concern at the private religion of James until he threatened their entrenched position by the rashness with which he attempted to force through the repeal of the Test Act and Penal Laws and the admission of dissenters and Roman Catholics to office. This alienated those who would have been his strongest adherents, so that when, in answer to an 'Invitation' sent by a small group of influential people, some Whigs, some Tories, known to history as the Immortal Seven, William of Orange landed at Torbay in November 1688 with an army of 15,000 veterans from the wars against Louis XIV, he met with virtually no opposition. James's army had been increased from 20,000 to about 30,000 since his accession, despite protests from prominent Tories in the 1685 Parliament, but part of it was in Ireland, and with Protestant officers in England refusing to act with

Roman Catholics it soon 'melted away'.[1] Many Tories, especially
in the west, welcomed William in the belief that he had come over
to bring his father-in-law to his senses, rather than to take the
crown. After the Revolution, most of them accepted him as king
de facto if not *de jure*, though driven into a false position by the
imposition of the oaths of abjuration by which the Whig Junto
endeavoured to drive them out of office. Although some leading
Tories engaged in plots with James and Louis XIV, and although
their belief in a foreign policy based on seapower rather than inter-
vention on the Continent conflicted with William's aims, he
resolutely refused to place himself in the power of one side only,
so that their party also enjoyed its share of Crown and Government
patronage at national and local level. Leading Tories in opposition
joined Whigs in opposition in the 1690s in an influential country
party, which secured the passing of the Triennial Act, of legislation
to reduce the number of placemen in Parliament, and secured the
disbandment of the army after the peace of Ryswick on the grounds
that the militia was the only constitutional force in peace time. The
whole Tory party rejoiced at the accession of Queen Anne, a devout
Anglican, whose heart, as she proclaimed was 'wholly English', but
she resolutely refused to make herself dependent on only one party,
and until just before her death resisted demands by Convocation
and by High Tories for an end to the practice of occasional con-
formity by which dissenters qualified for office by taking the
sacrament once in a while. They opposed bills to naturalise foreign
Protestants from 1709 to 1748 because, be they Dutch, German or
French, they were dissenters and invariably became Whigs once
they were in England.[2]

The system of mixed ministries had worked well enough to carry
the country through its immense war effort during Marlborough's
wars, even though the court party tended on occasions to fragment
on party lines. For this latter reason, the ablest party managers
would have liked single-party governments. Thomas, Marquis of

[1] J. R. Jones, *The Revolution of 1688* 289; C. Dalton, *English Army Lists and
Commission Registers* ii, pp. v, xxvii. For the general implications of the
Revolution, see J. P. Kenyon, *Revolution Principles*; Mark Goldie, 'Edmund
Bohun and *Jus Gentium* in the Revolution Debate 1689–93', *Historical Journal*
xx (1977) 569–86.

[2] See H. Horwitz, *Parliament, Policy and Politics in the Reign of William III*;
G. Holmes, *British Politics in the Age of Anne*; W. A. Speck, *Tory and Whig*.

Wharton, the greatest electoral magnate of his time, wanted Tories excluded from the Administration after the Whig victory at the 1708 election. Similarly, Henry St John, later Viscount Bolingbroke, could see little sense after 1710 in retaining in office Whigs who would not support the Government, while there were not enough places to go round for loyal supporters. This would have produced a two-party system, by which the Crown could call on one or the other to govern, and the organisation of the court party was certainly more efficient after 1715 under single-party ministries.

In the months which followed the death of Queen Anne in August 1714, the unforeseen happened. There was a ruthless purge of Tories from places apart from the very few who had life patents, and this was followed by a complete proscription which lasted forty-five years.[1]

During the last years of Queen Anne, overshadowed by the struggle for power between Robert Harley, Earl of Oxford, and Bolingbroke, the attitude of most of the Tories to the succession had been very Micawberlike, and they never really faced what would happen if the Queen died. Though the idea of the Hanoverian succession was distasteful to them and at best a necessary evil, the party was not mainly Jacobite and the figure of 80 Jacobites in the 1713–14 Parliament which has been given may be too high as it included some who had gone into opposition with Argyll.[2] Bolingbroke, who was more aware of possible danger in the event of the sudden death of the Queen, attempted in January 1714 to get James II's son, James the Old Pretender, to change or dissemble his religion, well knowing his party's traditional attachment to the Stuarts and their dislike of excluding the person nearest in line. James's refusal to do either put an end to further progress in this direction, while Oxford's flirtation with the court of Saint Germain seems to have been designed merely to get the Jacobite vote in Parliament. However, the Hanoverian envoys, reporting to the Electoral Prince (as the future George I was styled), represented the whole Tory party, apart from the small but influential group of Hanoverian Tories, as committed Jacobites and enemies to the Hanoverian succession. Another reason for George I's hatred of the Tories—the word is not too strong—is that they had long been

[1] *HC* i 62.
[2] Holmes 279.

represented as the friends of France, particularly at the time of the Exclusion Crisis and the renewal of hostilities with France in 1701, and he would not forgive them for what he regarded as their betrayal of the Allies at the peace of Utrecht and their refusal to pay arrears due to the Hanoverian troops in 1714. George I knew no English and depended on Baron Bothmer, a former Hanoverian envoy to London, as an intermediary, and it was Bothmer who advised him to employ only Whigs, who welcomed him with open joy, whereas the Tories, as the baron wrote in his diary, 'stood sullenly aside or even took the Stuart's part'.[1]

What took place in 1715 was not a change to an all-Whig ministry, it was a whole social revolution. Tory gentlemen could no longer provide for their younger sons in the traditional manner since places in the Army (the Navy was a partial exception), the Civil Service, or ecclesiastical livings in the gift of the Crown were denied to them. Tory army officers lost their commissions, sometimes without compensation, which was against all precedents. Tory lawyers could no longer become judges or K.C.s. The lower clergy, who were overwhelmingly Tory, could not become bishops, and resented the Whig bishops, who formed the most servile part of the House of Lords, and who acted, more often than not, as electoral agents for the Whigs in the constituencies, the most notorious being the Bishop of Lichfield who threatened his Tory chapter with ecclesiastical censure for incontinency if they would not vote for the Whig candidates at the 1727 election.[2] Tory merchants could no longer get government contracts, or directorships in the Bank of England or other great public companies. Moreover, many Tories, from old parliamentary families, could no longer afford to stand for Parliament, once deprived of office, that great restorer of men's estates. They were made to serve the expensive and troublesome office of sheriff in all but election years when Whigs were appointed to handle the writs, and likewise the Tories were excluded from the county lieutenancy. Though Tory Members were included in the commissions of the peace, they were swamped by Whig justices,

---

[1] See my article 'The Tories and the succession to the Crown in the 1714 Parliament', *Bulletin of the Institute of Historical Research* xlvi (1973) 176–85; R. Pauli, *Zeitschrift des Historischer Verein für Niedersachen* (1883) 83. I am grateful to Alex Hughes for translating a difficult passage in the diary.

[2] *HC* i 319.

often men of inferior rank in Tory counties.[1] Yet some historians have argued that the Tories did not want office under the first two Georges, mainly because some Tory knights of the shire did not want places after the fall of Walpole for fear of not being re-elected.[2] Of course they did not. Knights of the shire did not want to become placemen themselves under Queen Anne or George III either, but they wanted places for their relations and their dependants, and if Tories did not want office *per se*, why did they take it before 1715 and after 1760? The meaning of the proscription was put most eloquently by George Lyttelton in his *Letter to the Tories* (1747) in which he urged them to abandon Jacobitism:

We are kept out of all public employments of power and profit, and live like aliens and pilgrims in the land of our nativity; . . . no quality, no fortune, no eloquence, no learning, no wisdom, no probity is of any use to any man of our unfortunate denomination, ecclesiastic or layman, lawyer or soldier, peer or commoner, for obtaining the most deserved advancement in his profession, or any favour of the Crown; whilst, to our additional and insupportable vexation, the bare merit of hating us, and everything we love and hold sacred, daily advances dunces in the law and church, cowards in our fleets and armies, republicans in the King's house, and idiots everywhere!

Thus half the nation was driven into the wilderness—and the greater half, since Tories tended to represent counties and larger constituencies and would have won every general election between 1715 and 1747 had the number of seats obtained been commensurate with the number of votes cast. The Tory vote was remarkably steady as well as numerous, with little shift or splitting.[3] The point was put by Archibald Hutcheson, a Tory, who wrote to Sunderland:

The foundation is to make it a demonstration to the whole nation, that his Majesty relies on the affections of his people, as the only solid guarantee for the protestant succession; that he is equally the king of all his people, and that no part, much less the far greater part, may not lie under the impression that they are considered only in the

---

[1] Stuart mss. Box 1/299.

[2] John Owen, *The Rise of the Pelhams* 214; B. W. Hill, *The Growth of Parliamentary Parties 1689–1742*, 192–3.

[3] See polls in *HC* vol. i. I am indebted to Edward Johnson for giving me the results of his detailed work on poll books for the period.

nature of proscribed persons, and thereby irresistibly determined to lay hold of the first opportunity which shall offer, of freeing themselves from what they esteem an intolerable oppression.[1]

And by Bolingbroke, who wrote that a Prince who 'renders his sceptre the rod of one set of men, and the tool of another, will be esteemed by his subjects and by foreigners the King of half his people, that is half a King'.[2]

It was the proscription which turned the Tory party into a Jacobite one. Bolingbroke wrote to Sir William Wyndham: 'If milder measures had been pursued, certain it is that the Tories had never universally embraced Jacobitism. The violence of the Whigs forced them into the arms of the Pretender.'[3] This is confirmed by Iberville, the French ambassador, who knew Tory leaders and records many conversations with them, and who reported on 31 October 1714: 'I see that the number of the Jacobites, who before the death of the Queen was not by far as great as some believed, increase daily by the accession of all the Tories, moderate Jacobites or Hanoverians, moved by a violent rage against the King at their exclusion from office.'[4] A few Hanoverian Tories who had been offered places had refused them, as they would not break with their party. Early in 1715 he noted that the Prince of Wales (the future George II) seemed to hate the Tories as much as his father and that they seemed to be 'heading for civil war which they regard as their only resort'.[5] This was a counsel of despair at the purge, followed by the impeachment of Oxford and the driving into exile of Bolingbroke and Ormonde who joined the Pretender in France. The passing of the Riot Act after Jacobite riots all over England in the spring of 1715 was followed by the suspension of the Habeas Corpus Act, and by an increase in the army (from which Tories had been weeded out) to 15,200 in England and 12,000 in Ireland, as well as 6,000 Dutch troops which could be called upon under the Barrier Treaties. By August 1715, the French envoy described the Tories

[1] To Sunderland, 3 April 1722, Marlborough mss. from Blenheim, now in British Library.

[2] *Lyttelton Memoirs* i 196–7.

[3] *HC* i 62.

[4] AECP Ang. 265ff. 51. An example of an Hanoverian Tory who became a Jacobite is Sir Henry Bunbury (*HC* i 506–7).

[5] AECP Ang. 265ff. 70, 84.

as in a state of 'stupefaction and fear'.[1] They had been promised arms but no troops by Louis XIV, in the exhausted state of France, despite Bolingbroke's plea that a tenth of what the Prince of Orange had in 1688 would do, and when even that prospect had disappeared with Louis's death they would have abandoned any idea of rising had not the Scots started the rebellion without consulting the English.[2] To make matters worse, the plans in the west where the English rising was to be centred were betrayed by one of Ormonde's agents, thus enabling the Government to seize the ringleaders. The arrest of Members of Parliament, including Sir William Wyndham and Sir William Carew, and of peers like Lord Lansdowne, was notified to Parliament, but there were other preventive detentions in the west, most of them Tory Members of Anne's Parliaments. In the circumstances the Tories rather strove 'to smother their own contrivance than to bring it to bear'.[3] Lord Gower, who was said to have set out to join Thomas Forster, the leader of the rising in Northumberland, the day of Forster's defeat at Preston, went home when he learnt the news. Thereafter, Gower was always lampooned on this score.[4] Overconfidence and lack of secrecy had proved so disastrous that henceforth the Tories deliberately ridiculed in public any threat of a rising.[5] The other lesson they had learnt was that they needed regular troops.

In the diplomatic field too, the Whig government turned the tables on the Tories. France was then the greatest power in Europe as England became in the next century, and knowing that the greatest threat to the Hanoverian succession would come from there the Whig government negotiated an alliance with the Duke of Orleans, who had set aside the will of Louis XIV and assumed power as Regent on behalf of the young Louis XV. This was an amazingly bold step in view of the vilification of France as the arch-enemy by the Whigs ever since 1678. The negotiations, conducted between Stanhope and the Regent's favourite, Dubois, provided for the recognition of the Hanoverian succession and for the expulsion

---

[1] AECP Ang. 265ff. 158, 161.

[2] *HC* i 62; H. T. Dickinson, *Bolingbroke* 138–41.

[3] *HC* i 62; Morice mss. at the Bank of England, Walter Moyle to Humphry Morice, 26 Sept. 1715, and Sir N. Morice to Humphry Morice, 7 Oct. 1715.

[4] Stuart mss. 216/111; *Westminster Elections 1741–51*.

[5] G. G. Mounsey, *Carlisle in 1745* 25.

of the Pretender from France. Iberville, who was left out of them,
was still in London and was then an unhappy man. He reported in
1717 that his friends in the Tory party 'who have become almost all
Jacobites' reproached him with the ingratitude of France, and that
his windows were being broken in turn by Tory mobs, and by Whig
mobs who disapproved of the French alliance. Most of the Tories,
he added, blamed Oxford for everything that had happened.[1]
Bonet, the Prussian envoy, still thought that the Tories would
never accept the Pretender because he was a Roman Catholic, but
Bonet was a strong partisan of the Whigs and had no contacts
among the other side.[2] Even Oxford was so indignant at the harsh
treatment he had received from the House of Hanover (and he had
been chiefly instrumental in securing the passing of the Act of
Settlement in 1701) that he wrote to the Pretender from the Tower
in September 1716 offering his services.[3] Acting through Charles
Caesar, treasurer of the Navy under Queen Anne, and William
Bromley, secretary of state under the late Queen, who like Caesar
corresponded with the Pretender, Oxford directed the Swedish Plot
of 1716–17. This was a plan for a new rising if Charles XII of
Sweden, who was determined to revenge himself on George I for
having as Elector of Hanover taken advantage of his difficulties to
dispossess him of Bremen and Verden, would assist by sending
troops. Money was collected in England to pay for their use in
bringing about a restoration. In January 1717, the English Government, against all diplomatic practice, seized the papers of Gyllenborg, the Swedish envoy.[4] In one of these, Gyllenborg said that the
Pretender derived the strength of his party from his being English
whereas George I was a foreigner, and without that the Pretender
would have had few supporters however strong his hereditary
claims.[5] Charles XII's death, followed by the failure of a Spanish
expedition under Ormonde at the beginning of 1719, put an end for
the time being to any prospect of help from abroad.[6]

[1] AECP Ang. 293ff. 25, 34; 294ff. 13–14.
[2] Hill 138.
[3] Lord Mahon, *History of England from the Peace of Utrecht 1713–1783* (1858
ed.) i 279.
[4] *HC* i 63.
[5] *Letters which passed between Count Gyllenborg, the Barons Görtz, Sparre and
others*, London 1717, 23.
[6] *HC* i 63.

The widespread discontent in England caused by the burst of the South Sea Bubble seemed to present an opportunity to the Tories. Sunderland, George I's prime minister, seeking Tory votes to save himself from impeachment, and to safeguard his future since he had no hopes from the Prince of Wales in the event of the death of George I, made large promises to the Tories. Bromley was against dealing with Sunderland, and Oxford, who was out of the Tower but in retirement, was not consulted. Atterbury, Bishop of Rochester and Dean of Westminster since Queen Anne's days, as the Pretender's chief representative in England dealt with Sunderland mainly through Archibald Hutcheson, an able Tory lawyer who administered Ormonde's affairs in England. What Sunderland was asked for at first was a free Parliament, that is one elected without any Crown or Government pressure on elections. This had been the universal request at the Restoration and at the Revolution of 1688, and what the *English Advice to the Freeholders of England*, distributed by the Tories at the 1715 election, had called for. It would seem that Sunderland tried to oblige, for according to a report from the Jacobite agent in London, at a meeting of the Cabinet in February 1722, with George I presiding, Sunderland—

> opposed the buying the ensuing elections, that it was a method very expensive, which the present situation of affairs could not dispense with, so that it was impossible for the Treasury to hold out by procuring pliable persons to be elected, who after they were chosen must be maintained with places and pensions etc. . . . Mr Walpole asked with some heat if his Lordship was bringing in the Tories and having a Tory Parliament? To this the Earl [Sunderland] replied that the Tories and the Whigs were equally entitled to a share in the Administration, and that he was not for governing by brigades. King George stared the Earl of Sunderland in the face at the name of a Tory Parliament, for it seems nothing is so hideous and frightful to him as a Tory.

With the apparent connivance of Sunderland, the Tories then entered into a scheme for a rising in each county, assisted by the Irish regiments in the French service and those under Ormonde in Spain. The plan was revealed by Dubois to Walpole and Townshend the day of Sunderland's death, 19 April 1722.[1] Walpole's way of

[1] *HC* i 63–5, 494; Archibald Hutcheson, 28 and 30 July 1721, 23 April 1722,

handling the Atterbury plot was to terrify the Tories by bills of pains and penalties against the underlings while taking no proceedings against the Members of Parliament or peers named in it apart from Atterbury himself. This was so successful that afterwards, the Tories, who still formed the bulk of the Opposition, hardly dared attend Parliament 'thinking it better to lie still and to give no provocation'.[1]

It was in this situation that Bolingbroke, who never forgave the Pretender for dismissing him for negligence in failing to send over any arms during the '15 rebellion, and who had succeeded in detaching his friend Sir William Wyndham from the Stuart court, returned to England having obtained a pardon by bribing the Duchess of Kendall, George I's mistress. Although he was never able to live down his past, although he, one of the greatest orators of his time, was deprived of a voice in the Lords, his sheer intelligence and restless energy enabled him to play a crucial part behind the scenes. His first step was to make overtures to Walpole on behalf of three Tory leaders who were his friends, Lord Bathurst, Lord Gower and Sir William Wyndham, explaining that they were 'ready to enter into any measures' with Walpole and Townshend, being 'desirous to rid themselves of the disagreeable situation they were in by renouncing Jacobitism'. Next year, having got nowhere with Walpole and carrying with him his friend Wyndham, Bolingbroke allied himself with Pulteney, the head of the new Whig opposition, with a view to forming a coalition of the two opposition parties to bring down Walpole.[2] On the accession of George II in 1727, the Tories, who had been in the wilderness for twelve years, hoped for a change of heart from the new king. Charles Caesar reported to the Pretender on 27 June:

> Some of the Tories, particularly such as Lord Bolingbroke would influence, had shown an inclination to quit their principles in hopes of preferment, and upon the Duke of Hanover's death and his son's succeeding him, your steady friends found that many more would do the same, they could not tell where it would stop, they thought that

---

Marlborough mss. For Atterbury's part in the plot, see also G. V. Bennett, *The Tory Crisis in Church and State.*

[1] *HC* i 65–6.

[2] Dickinson, 140–2; *HC* i 66–7.

the only way to prevent a considerable breach amongst the Tories upon this occasion was to go one and all to court.

George II, however, was no more inclined to employ them than his father had been. They were divided among themselves, Wyndham as 'the head of those who called themselves Hanoverian Tories' supporting a coalition with the opposition Whigs, which was opposed by William Shippen and the 'veteran staunch Jacobites'.[1] To some Whig contemporaries at this time the number of true Jacobites did seem small.[2] Repeated disappointments had brought despair. The identity of the party seemed lost in the coalition, and the Tories now read the *Craftsman*, which preached that the only real distinction was between Patriots and a corrupt Administration, and that party distinctions had ceased to matter.[3] Political realities were very different. The belief of some historians that Wyndham led the bulk of the Tories who were loyal to the House of Hanover, while Shippen led a group of about fifty Jacobites, does not stand up to a close examination of the politics of the time.[4] There is very little evidence that Shippen led a party within a party, and the expression which is most frequently applied to him in reports of parliamentary proceedings is 'Shippen alone'. Wyndham owed his position in Parliament to being the best speaker on the Tory side and to the advice of his friend Bolingbroke, who was surpassed as a parliamentary strategist only by Walpole, but he had few personal followers. Speaker Onslow wrote that Wyndham—

formed such a new set of principles with regard to the public, and from them grew to think that the religion and liberties of the nation so much depended on the support of the present family to the throne, that he lost all confidence with the Jacobites and the most rigid of the Tories, and it is thought would have left them entirely if he could have stood the reproach of that in his county or could have maintained a prevailing interest there without them; and upon that footing would willingly have come into a new Whig Administration upon the exclusion of Sir Robert Walpole, with whom he would never have acted, and with the admission of some few of his Tory friends who in

[1] *HC* i 67.
[2] *Lord Hervey's Memoirs*, ed. Romney Sedgwick, i 3–5.
[3] Stuart mss. Box 1/299.
[4] Coxe, *Sir Robert Walpole* i 294; Hill 192–3; Owen 214.

company with him would willingly also have left their party for such a change.[1]

Wyndham's strategy of uniting with the discontented Whigs was deeply distasteful to the Tories, who again and again refused to act with the Whigs in opposition, and had not succeeded in ending the proscription. Nor was his zeal for the House of Hanover sincere, as we shall see. In 1730 the Tories suddenly appeared 'in perfect coalition' with the Whig opposition. This was brought about by a circular letter from the Pretender sent through Ormonde urging his friends in Parliament to 'unite in the measures against the Government and even with those who oppose it for different views than theirs', especially those 'which tend to promote a misunderstanding between the English Government and any foreign power, but most especially France'. In the short term it was linked with the attack on the Government for allowing the French to restore the port of Dunkirk contrary to the terms of the Peace of Utrecht. In the long term, it was connected with the arrival in Rome in January 1731 of Lord Cornbury, the great-grandson of Lord Chancellor Clarendon, to whom Bolingbroke was to dedicate his *Letters on History*. In secret meetings with the Pretender, he elaborated a plan for a restoration by offering places to leading Whigs and Tories in opposition. The project was directed on the English side by Lord Arran (Ormonde's brother), Lord Strafford, Lord Bathurst and Lord Gower, while Cornbury went on to Paris to negotiate with Chauvelin, the French foreign minister, who favoured a more aggressive foreign policy than the chief minister Cardinal Fleury, whom it was thought he would succeed.[2] In London, the French envoy Chavigny, a protégé of Chauvelin, had several meetings with Bolingbroke and Wyndham with whom he was on the closest terms. Chavigny reported in 1732–3 that they had told him that the Tories could not reconcile themselves to the Hanoverian succession and wanted a free Parliament. They thought that the Hanoverian family was as unpopular as ever. Looking on the character of the Pretender as a major obstacle to a restoration, Bolingbroke set his sights on Charles Edward, the Young Pretender, then twelve years old, who

[1] *HC* ii 563.
[2] *HC* ii 164; for Chauvelin and French policy under Fleury see P. Vaucher, *Walpole et la politique de Fleury*.

was regarded as forward as well as handsome, and whose portrait was everywhere in London. He then elaborated a plan for the education of Charles Edward and his younger brother Henry, saying that if he and Wyndham 'could but get hold of the children' there was nothing they could not do with the Tories.[1] Bolingbroke intervened directly by sending his secretary Brinsden to Paris with a proposal that James should resign his claims to his eldest son Charles Edward, who was to be educated as a Protestant under Ormonde in Switzerland or France. The Pretender refused to comply point blank.[2] Cardinal Fleury, however, was a peace-loving old man, who used Chauvelin as a bogey but kept him on a tight rein, and he was still on close terms with Horatio Walpole,[3] Sir Robert's brother, who had been British ambassador at Paris and still expressed feelings of the warmest friendship for the old Cardinal. Lord Orrery observed that while 'the duty of every Englishman to hate the King of France' was preached as the 'eleventh commandment', 'we are at present like wooden puppets, squeaking, strutting and acting solely for the machination and dexterity of the nimble fingered Cardinal'.[4] Walpole did not rely on Fleury's goodwill alone. Sniffing something in the wind, he had made overtures to Col. William Cecil, the Jacobite agent in England and a kinsman of Orrery and the Earl of Exeter. Under the guise of seeking his advice, Walpole flattered Cecil into meeting him alone. Cecil always denied having revealed anything of importance, but Walpole certainly learnt of Bolingbroke's plan, and Cecil was hopelessly compromised.[5] Disheartened with what he regarded as French breach of faith and accusations from the Tories of having disclosed the secret of his negotiations to his friend Bolingbroke, Cornbury broke his connexion with the Pretender in 1735.[6] The same year Bolingbroke withdrew to France, living at Chanteloup in Touraine.[7]

---

[1] Dickinson, 232; AECP Ang. 376ff. 247–73; 377ff. 126–31; 379f. 164; 330ff. 205–7, 228.

[2] Stuart mss. 157/29; 158/156.

[3] To avoid repeating 'old' and 'young' Horace Walpole, Walpole's brother has been called Horatio Walpole and his son Horace Walpole throughout.

[4] *Orrery Papers* i 105–6.

[5] Stuart mss. 144/6; Horace Walpole, *Memoirs of the Reign of George II* i 73. For Cecil see *HC* i App. pp. 113–14; for Orrery, see next chapter.

[6] *HC* ii 164.

[7] *Lyttelton Memoirs* i 63.

2

War with Spain and the Fall of Walpole

Bolingbroke, Horace Walpole wrote,

> who had sowed a division in the Pretender's court, by the scheme for
> the father's resigning his claim to the eldest boy, repeated the same
> plan of discord here, on the first notion of the Prince's disgusts; and
> the whole Opposition was instructed to offer their services to the
> Heir Apparent against the Crown and the Minister.[1]

Though Bolingbroke and Wyndham could not afford to separate
themselves from the Tories, without whom they would have been
generals without troops, the party could and did differ from them.
When in 1737 the Prince of Wales decided to apply to Parliament for
an increased allowance, Wyndham said 'that he would answer for his
whole party, as well as for himself; that he was very happy that an
occasion presented itself to convince his Royal Highness, by their
zealous and hearty appearance in support of his interest, how far
they were from being Jacobites and how much they were misrepresented under that name'; but in the event, though he spoke he
did not vote for the application, on which 45 Tories abstained, with
the result that it was defeated by a majority of 30, an example of what
Bolingbroke called 'the absurd behaviour of the Tories, which no
experience can cure'.[2] Next year an attempt by the Prince to come to
terms with the Tories broke down on Wyndham's stipulation that
'the Prince's people should join in reducing the army'. In the ensuing
debate on the army estimates political realities came through the
constitutional proprieties. Lord Noel Somerset, brother of the 3rd
Duke of Beaufort, who was regarded as 'the rising head of the Tory

[1] *Memoirs of the Reign of George II* i 73.
[2] *HC* i 68–9.

interest',[1] pointed out that the people of England were 'totally unaccustomed to military discipline and unprovided with arms'. Supposing they could be overawed by 'a large mercenary army' and that an administration could get control of both Houses of Parliament by corrupt means, then 'by the Revolution principles, it would be very lawful to resist such a government; but if it had a standing army to support it, they could not be able.' Replying, Walpole declared:

> No man of common prudence will profess himself openly a Jacobite; by so doing he not only may injure his private fortune, but he must render himself less able to do any effectual service to the cause he has embraced; therefore, there are but few such men in the kingdom. Your right Jacobite, Sir, disguises his true sentiments, he roars out for revolution principles; he pretends to be a great friend to liberty . . . These are the men we have most reason to be afraid of: they are, I am afraid, more numerous than most gentlemen imagine, and I wish I could not say they have been lately joined, and very much assisted by some gentlemen, who, I am convinced, have always been, and still are, very sincere and true friends to our present happy establishment. By the accession of these new allies, as I may justly call them, the real but concealed Jacobites have succeeded even beyond their own expectation; and therefore I am not ashamed to say I am in fear of the Pretender.

Pointing out that if the Pretender landed at the head of five or six thousand men 'there is no question but that they would meet with many, especially of the meaner sort, to join them', he went on to say that the army was also needed to suppress the smugglers as the local militia, in most cases, co-operated with rather than acted against them, an interesting fact in view of the close connexion between the smugglers and the Jacobites.[2] It obviously served Walpole's turn to brand all Tories as Jacobites, and to tar their Whig allies with the same brush for acting with them. Walpole was certainly obsessed with the danger of Jacobitism at home and abroad, and this concern has been thought akin to paranoia. But it was the sort of madness which kept him one jump ahead! Obviously, since any expression of Jacobitism, indeed any opposition to the Hanoverian succession,

[1] Dr Linda Colley, 'The Loyal Brotherhood and the Cocoa Tree', *Historical Journal* xx (1977) 81.

[2] *HC* i 68–9; *Parl. Hist.* x 375–467.

was treason, punishable by death and loss of estates, he had no means of knowing exactly how strong it was. But by a widespread and costly intelligence system at home and abroad, he was able to defeat most Jacobite schemes.[1] Conversations recorded in the diary of Sir Dudley Ryder, the attorney general, one of the most important new sources for the period, show that Walpole really believed the Tories were Jacobites, and this is confirmed by his brother Horatio and his son Horace.

While correspondence between leading Tories and the Pretender, always a risky business even if conducted in cypher, had fallen off since there was no positive plan afoot, the flow of funds from England sent anonymously through the Pretender's bankers in Paris continued. Nor had the Tories ceased to turn their sights towards the Stuart princes. A Frenchman who was in Rome in 1739 reported that it was well known there that the Pretender was getting large sums of money from England. The English who flocked to Rome, he wrote, were eager to see the Prince of Wales and the Duke of York, as the Stuart princes were styled, and since going to the Stuart palace was a capital offence in English law they asked him and other foreigners where the princes would appear in public in order to meet them.[2] That Jacobitism was not extinct was shown on the outbreak of the war with Spain in 1739. In the City of London, the common council on which the Tories had a majority led by Humphrey Parsons, a Tory alderman who was twice lord mayor of London and a zealous Jacobite, joined the friends of Frederick Prince of Wales there and on the court of aldermen, in fanning the agitation for war by petitions and addresses. Commenting on these proceedings, Walpole told Dudley Ryder that 'the disaffected are endeavouring to get the city into declarations and addresses that may distress us', which, he added 'did its mischief at once, in that such a thing as this came to the court of Rome and other foreign courts as the sense of the people for the Pretender, and that they want nothing but a standard and 5,000 men to begin with'. Though Whigs and

[1] See P. Fritz, *Jacobitism and the English Ministers*; and below, chapters 3 and 4.

[2] Receipts from England through Waters in Paris for sums usually between £100–£300 occur in most volumes of the Stuart mss.; Charles de Brosses, *L'Italie il y a cent ans, ou Lettres écrites d'Italie à quelques amis en 1739 et 1740*, ed. Columb., ii 93–100.

Tories in opposition were united in pressing for war, they did so for different reasons. Walpole told Ryder in October 1739 that there was—

> a great difference between the Jacobites and the patriot Whigs, particularly those of the Prince's court; and they had a meeting in the vacation when one of the Prince's friends proposed a revolution in favour of the Prince, saying that the King's interest was entirely lost, and he could not support it, but the Jacobites said if there was to be an alteration, it should be a restoration. This broke off the treaty. He assured me this was told him by one present at the meeting.[1]

Pulteney at this time thought Bolingbroke's counsels obnoxious, and was particularly critical of the fiasco of the secession on the Spanish Convention moved by Wyndham, whereby most of the Opposition left Parliament.[2]

The Scots took the initiative to secure a restoration. On the outbreak of the war with Spain, seven Scottish lords formed an association and issued an Invitation to James Stuart on the model of that sent to William of Orange in 1688. They were the Duke of Perth, his uncle Lord John Drummond, Lord Lovat, Lord Linton (who in 1741 became Earl of Traquair), his brother Hon. John Stewart, Donald Cameron the younger of Lochiel, and Sir James Campbell of Auchenbreck. Their secretary was William Macgregor of Balhaldy, the chief of the outlawed clan Macgregor, who was a cousin of Lochiel and an intimate of Lovat's. The disastrous consequences of having started the rebellion in Scotland in 1715 without consulting the English was always present in James's mind, and he replied that nothing could be done in Scotland without co-operation from his friends in England, and that France must be approached with a request for arms and regular troops. The English had in fact made strong objections to a purely Scottish project, as an enclosure in the correspondence of Murray of Broughton, the Jacobite agent in Scotland, states:

> The King [the Pretender] is informed, that his friends in England being apprehensive that some project might be forming in Scotland,

[1] *HC* i 69–70; ii 282, 326–7.
[2] *Marchmont Papers*, ed. Rose, ii 179–80.

for his restoration, without an attempt being made in England and by consequence without a sufficient prospect of success, his said English friends had advised those in Scotland not to proceed in any such project without hearing from the King. That no project should be examined in which both nations have not their share and will himself never authorise or agree to any that hath not a reasonable prospect of success.[1]

In order to ascertain the intentions of his leading supporters in England, James sent Col. Arthur Brett, an experienced army officer who, on the accession of George I, had been dismissed as lieutenant-colonel of the regiment which became the Royal Welch Fusiliers.[2] Those Brett dealt with were Lord Orrery, Sir John Cotton, Sir Watkin Williams Wynn, Lord Barrymore, and William Shippen. John Boyle, 5th Earl of Orrery [I], also sat in the English House of Lords as Baron Boyle. He had large estates in co. Cork, including Rathgoggan and the borough of Charleville, but lived mainly in England at Marston near Frome in Somerset. He had inherited his father's literary tastes, and moved in the circles of Pope and Swift. The friend and correspondent of Lord Barrymore and Dr King, the Jacobite principal of St. Mary's Hall, Oxford, he much admired Thomas Carte's Life of the first Duke of Ormonde, which he regarded as 'the first and best history of those times that has yet appeared'. He had made his maiden speech in the Lords in 1732 against the standing army, which he called 'an emblem of distrust between his Majesty and his subjects', and answered a whip from Col. William Cecil for the Lords early in 1739 when he spoke strongly against the Spanish Convention. Politically, he was a strong opponent of Walpole and had dealings with Chesterfield and Boling-broke as well as with the Stuart court.[3] Sir John Hynde Cotton, 3rd Bt., Member for Cambridge and a Lord of Trade under Queen Anne, was descended from an old Cambridgeshire family who had acquired the manor of Madingley near Cambridge by marriage, and was the head of the Tory party in that county. His predominant interest at Cambridge, however, was weakened by a series of expensive contests. He lost the allegiance of the corporation as soon as they

---

[1] Stuart mss. 209/7; *Memorials of Murray of Broughton* 364.

[2] Dalton, *Army Lists* vi 101, 197, 341.

[3] *Orrery Papers* i xii–xix, 111, 133, 176, 183, 193, 231–2, 252–3, 256, 264–6, 287, 301–2, 320.

realised he was not spending quite as much in the borough as he used to, and he transferred in 1741 to Marlborough the pocket borough of a Tory peer. Described by William Cole, the Cambridge antiquary, as 'one of the tallest, biggest, fattest men I have ever seen', he had to have a special set of chairs made at Madingley to take his weight. 'He was supposed,' Cole wrote, 'to be able to drink as much wine as any man in England without being disgusted by it', saying, on being told that it would be better for his gouty leg if he drank less, that 'if it would not bear his usual allowance of six bottles it was no leg to him'. Dr King, as well as Cole, was a frequent visitor to Madingley, where Cotton gave a home to Thomas Carte, who catalogued his library, including the greatest collection of pamphlets on the civil war then in existence. Cotton was related to the Wogans, Jacobite exiles, several of whom were in James's service. In Parliament, Cotton was the best speaker on the Tory side next to Wyndham. 'He had wit,' Horace Walpole wrote, 'and the faithful attendant on wit, ill nature, and was the greatest master of the arts of the House, where he seldom made but short speeches, having a stammering in his elocution, which, however, he knew how to manage with humour.'[1]

Sir Watkin Williams Wynn, 3rd Bt., Member of Parliament for Denbighshire, was the grandson of Sir William Williams, Speaker of the House of Commons under Charles II and solicitor-general to James II, who purchased a large estate at Llanvorda across the border into Shropshire and married the heiress to Glascoed in Denbighshire. Acquiring Plasyward in the same county through his mother, he inherited, on the death of his first wife's father, Llwydiarth and Glanllyn in Montgomeryshire and Llangedwin in Denbighshire, and the next year succeeded to Wynnstay, which he made his seat, as well as Rhiwgoch in Merioneth under the will of his mother's cousin Sir John Wynn, whose name he assumed. His vast estates, great electioneering activity, and personal popularity soon made him the head of the North Wales Tories, and such a dominating figure in Welsh politics that he was called 'Prince of Wales'. In preparation for an expected county election in 1720 he came at the head of 500 horsemen and wrote: 'To-morrow I roast a very large ox and hind, and intend to drink the town of Wrexham

[1] *HC* i 201, 584; Lady A. Houblon, *Houblon Family*, ii 36–40, 112–13; J. Nichols, *Literary Anecdotes of the 18th Century* ii 480–1.

dry.' At the time of the 1722 election and the Atterbury plot he and his friend Lord Bulkeley 'audaciously burnt the King's picture and the several pictures of all the royal family'. Wynn was the leading member of the Cycle of the White Rose, a secret Welsh Jacobite society whose membership extended into Cheshire and Lancashire, and he helped his fellow members Sir Robert Grosvenor and Lord Barrymore (who was his life-long friend) in their elections. At the 1732 election, when Grosvenor was under violent attack from Government supporters, Wynn came to the rescue accompanied by his liveried servants and 900 colliers from Wrexham. When he was elected mayor of Chester in 1736, the *Gentleman's Magazine* reported that 'the feasting continued several days, in so much that little business was done but by cooks and confectioners. Such appearance of gentlemen were never seen since Lord Delamere was mayor at the Revolution.' Nor was Wynn's popularity confined to his own part of the country, for when he came up to London to attend Parliament, Welshmen came out as far as Finchley and escorted him to town in a great procession. George Kelly, Ormonde's secretary, whom Wynn had financially supported during his imprisonment in the Tower as one of the chief agents in the Atterbury plot, wrote to the Pretender in 1737 that Wynn ought to be consulted before Charles Edward was sent on any foreign travels.[1]

James Barry, 4th Earl of Barrymore [I], Member for Wigan, had been a colonel of foot under Queen Anne serving with distinction in Spain, where he first became connected with the Duke of Argyll. He had a seat at Castlelyons in co. Cork and large estates in the same county, and got a fortune of £10,000 by his first wife, a sister of Charles Boyle, 2nd Earl of Burlington. His second wife, with whom he eloped in 1706 when her father, Earl Rivers, opposed the match, was a great heiress, and by 1721 Barrymore had managed to get possession of all the Rivers estates in Lancashire, Cheshire, Yorkshire and Essex, and control of one seat at Wigan. Like his kinsman and friend Lord Orrery, he did not live in Ireland but in England, at the Rivers' houses of Rock Savage and Marbury in Cheshire and Wardley in Lancashire. He had lost his regiment on the accession of

[1] *HC* ii 543–4; P. D. G. Thomas, 'Jacobitism in Wales', *Welsh History Review* i (No. 3) (1962) 288–95 and 'Wynnstay versus Chirk Castle', *National Library of Wales Journal* xi (No. 2) (1959) 105–23; A. Roberts, *Wynnstay and the Wynns* 9–11; Stuart mss. 194/10.

George I and never forgave the House of Hanover, though he decided against joining the '15 rebellion after the arrest of the West Country Jacobites. In Parliament he was a fairly frequent speaker and attended regularly, writing at the time of the split in the Whig party in 1717:

> Nobody has more thorough contempt for ministers and what is called men in great offices than I have. I cannot remember they ever did true service to their country, they minded indeed strengthening themselves to carry on private piques and getting as much money as they could, but I have observed that when such people fall out, now and then some good come on it, so it may prove now; for which reason I would not be absent at this juncture. It may be in a man's vote at this time to do some good which, perhaps, may never again be in his power.[1]

Shippen, a wealthy lawyer not a great landowner, had mellowed with age and took no considerable part in Jacobite affairs after this time. Such were the principal Pretender's friends in England. They were committed Jacobites, but had a great deal to lose—some, a very great deal to lose.

A report to the Pretender on these negotiations dated 28 March 1740 stated:

> Col. Brett found the King's [the Pretender's] friends more timorous and backward than heretofore, and as full of good inclinations as ever. It was absolutely impossible to form any plan of business with them; they shudder at the thought of an attempt when it can be compassed, and yet wish it, and even seem to long for it ... Lord Orrery has been all the winter in Ireland but left word that he would return if the King should think fit. Mr. Shippen trembles ... Sir John Hynde Cotton doubts, or seems to doubt of others, but answers clearly for himself; Watkin Williams is hearty and may certainly be depended on. The gentry, yeomanry, commonalty are well disposed, better than ever for a restoration. The City of London is full of spirit and gives effectual proofs of it; but with all this it is impossible to bring them into any measures that can give sufficient encouragement to any foreign minister.[2]

---

[1] SP 44/104/46; *HC* i 440. M. Cox, 'Sir Roger Bradshaigh and the electoral management of Wigan', *Bulletin of John Rylands Library* xxxvii. 120–64; Lodge, *Irish Peerage* i 309–12.

[2] Stuart mss. 221/109 and 131.

The chief reasons for their backwardness, was said to be 'the Duke of Hanover's [George II's] violence, Walpole's vigilance, the present appearance of an army and a fleet, a long series of disappointments, and a confirmed habit of despondence and indolence'. Shippen, in fact, proved 'so weak upon the prospect of real business' that he was left out of the consultations altogether. The others, Brett reported, declared they would 'not fail to join such troops as the King of France shall send to their assistance'. Cotton agreed to remain in London in order to settle 'a correspondence with proper persons in different parts of England by messengers without trusting anything to writing'. Everything depended upon whether France would provide regular troops.[1] A memorandum in the French Foreign Office says that at this time persons of the greatest distinction, gentlemen and noblemen, came over from England to see Cardinal Fleury asking for assistance, but as nothing was put in writing by Fleury, we do not know who they were except for Lord Barrymore, who wrote to the Pretender from Paris 12/23 May 1740:

> Your faithful servants think by many incidents lately happened that the present juncture is much the most favourable that has been for many years, and if anything can be had from this side, I should not fear of success, but to make any attempt, unless a sufficient force was at hand to resort to, would only add strength to your enemies and certain ruin to your Majesty's friends; what can be expected from hence I fear are only fair words, I wish I may be deceived, but am sure I succeeded in demonstrating the feasibleness of the undertaking.[2]

Barrymore asked the Pretender to destroy the original of his letter; this was done, but a copy was kept. These developments were not to the liking of Bolingbroke, who wrote to Wyndham:

> Of all the causes of our present public misfortunes, which are easy to be traced, a principal one is this: the Whigs have always looked on the protestant succession, and the Tories on the restoration of the Stuarts, as sure means to throw the whole power of the government into the hands of one or the other of them, and to keep it there: the former were encouraged and confirmed by the weak conduct of my Lord Oxford; by the characters of the late and present King, different

[1] Stuart mss. 222/33 and 107; 223/129.
[2] J. Colin, *Louis XV et les Jacobites* 12–13; *HC* i 440; Stuart mss. 222/128.

indeed, but suited to their purpose; and by the absurd behaviour of the Tories, which no experience can cure.[1]

Wyndham suddenly arrived in Paris in the spring of 1740, first to confer with his friend Bolingbroke, and then on to see Cardinal Fleury. Col. Daniel O'Brian, the Pretender's representative at the French court and one of the army officers who had lost his commission in 1715, wrote: 'Though Lord Bolingbroke's behaviour has been all along such as you know, and though Sir William Wyndham's has been for some time very unaccountable, yet they both seem to dread any business of the King's should be thought of without them.'[2] On Wyndham's death in June, George Lyttelton, a leading member of the Whig opposition and a protégé of his kinsman Lord Cobham, wrote:

> His influence with the Tories was the only means of keeping that party in any system of rational measures. Now he is gone . . . it is much to be feared that resentment, despair, and inability of conducting themselves may drive the Tories back into their old prejudices, heat and extravagance.[3]

In other words, they might not so easily be persuaded to play the game of the Whig opposition, and in a different international situation, might play their own under the new leadership of Cotton and Wynn. On his side, Walpole had not been inactive. He made overtures to Thomas Carte, the historian, in 1739–40 through Avery, a London merchant and a supposed Jacobite, telling Carte he was averse to the shedding of blood and asking him to procure assurances in James's own hand for the maintenance of the constitution in Church and State and the safe retreat of the Hanoverian family. A clergyman who had become a nonjuror on the accession of George I, Carte had been secretary to Bishop Atterbury at the time of the plot and was said to have stirred up Jacobite riots at the Coventry election of 1722. Pursued by the King's messengers, he had made his escape to France in 1723, but had returned to England about 1730 when Queen Caroline obtained leave for him to do so, a favour of which

[1] Coxe, *Sir Robert Walpole* iii 524.
[2] Stuart mss. 221/178. For O'Brian's career under Anne, see C. G. T. Dean, *The Royal Hospital, Chelsea*, 183, 190.
[3] *HC* i 70.

he availed himself but which he had not solicited. He was at the centre of Tory politics, living with Sir John Cotton at Madingley, and received grants from the common council of London, the Goldsmiths' and the Vintners' Companies towards his history of England (of which the first volume only was completed before his death). His letters in the Stuart papers give some of the best reports of parliamentary debates, the details of which he obtained directly from Cotton or from his friend Sir John St. Aubyn, knight of the shire for Cornwall, and of the proceedings of the corporation of London, told him by his friends Sir John Barber and Humphrey Parsons, both of them aldermen and lords mayor. The Pretender gave him such a letter as Walpole had requested, adding: 'as for the Princes of the House of Hanover, I thank God I have no resentment against them, nor against any one living.' Carte then handed over to Walpole James's letter, which the minister asked to keep. Suddenly Carte found himself being threatened: 'He put me in mind that the warrant against me was not called in but still lay in the messenger's hands', whereupon he protested that he had come at Walpole's invitation. The minister then tried another tack. Saying he knew Carte was poor, he offered him a handsome annuity or the deanery of Windsor in exchange for information. When Carte refused indignantly, Walpole laughed, saying how could he 'learn the Jacobites' designs but from the Jacobites themselves?' He then saw Carte to the door with every courtesy and advised him to have nothing to do in future with such men as Avery.[1] When Walpole attempted to continue his 'negotiations' with James, the latter replied that if Walpole was in earnest let him send his son (Horace), who was due to go on the grand tour, and he would talk to him! Carte was regarded as 'honest and zealous, but indiscreet', but it was thought better to let Carte and Cecil 'go on, because both Sir Robert Walpole and Lord Ilay [brother of Argyll and Walpole's manager for Scottish elections] were apprised of all their motions, and seemed to believe that the King [James] had no other correspondents'.[2] In

[1] Nichols, *Literary Anecdotes* ii 471–518; Robert Digby to William, Lord Digby, 18 Nov. 1722, Digby papers formerly in the possession of Miss Fiona Digby. AEM & D Ang. 76ff. 73–92; Vaucher, App. ii pp. 455–8; Lord Mahon lii–liii.

[2] Stuart mss. 219/111 and 148; 253/154; James Browne, *History of the Highlands* (1852–3 ed.) ii 458, 468–9.

any case, while Cardinal Fleury lived there was no real prospect of a restoration with French assistance. Walpole knew this, telling Ryder 'France would certainly not go into a war with us during the life of the Cardinal, but after his death, he believed she would, for the majority of the council were for it'.[1] He was absolutely right.

Co-operation between the two wings of the Opposition had virtually ceased with the death of Wyndham. The motion for the dismissal of Walpole in February 1741, Carte reported,

> was set on foot by the Duke of Argyll and the party of the Old Whigs without either concerting measures with the Tories or acquainting them with the matter, so that when it was moved in the Commons, Sir John Hynde Cotton and Sir Watkin Williams were forced to go about the House to solicit their friends to stay the debate, which they were vexed should be brought on without their concurrence

whereupon 'Parsons, Lord Mayor, and most of the Tory party left the House', including Shippen who 'retired into Solomon's porch, and would not vote either way'. Oxford's son Edward Lord Harley and his nephew Edward Harley left the House. Carte went on:

> Had all Sir Robert Walpole's actual opposers stayed he would not have carried the question by above 50 votes but the retiring of so many encouraged others to stay and even vote for him who durst not else have done it. Among those who voted were Lord Cornbury, Lord Quarendon the Earl of Lichfield's son, Mr. Bathurst, son of the Lord of that name, and Lord Andover, son of the Earl of Berkshire, though the fathers of the last three voted against Sir Robert Walpole in the Lords.[2]

It is a fact that at this time most Tories preferred Walpole to their Whig allies in Opposition. After his ruthlessness at the time of the Atterbury plot, he had gone out of his way to conciliate them by being more Anglican than the Church party, defeating the efforts of the Whig dissenters to secure the repeal of the Test and Corporation Acts, though this was of course to prevent them raising the cry of 'the Church in danger', their most effective call to battle in Anne's

[1] *HC* i 70.
[2] Stuart mss. 232/13; *HMC Egmont diary* iii 192.

days.[1] Shippen did not conceal his dislike of the opposition Whigs, saying: 'Robin and I are two honest men; he is for King George and I for King James; but those men with the long cravats [meaning Sandys and his associates] only desire places, either under King George or King James', and gave as his reason for walking out that 'he would not pull down Robin upon republican principles'. The motion was also disliked by the Tories because their 'principles abhor even the shadow of bills of pains and penalties', and this applied particularly to the Harleys because of Oxford's sufferings under such a bill.[2] There were also political reasons, since the Tories

> were not to be employed, they had rather Sir Robert was at the head of affairs than that the malcontent Whigs should take his place, of whose warmth they had less opinion than of Sir Robert's coolness, whose personal behaviour towards the Tories has always been obliging although an enemy to them as a party, and . . . they had too much pride to be the tools of the discontented Whigs, and put their hand under the stirrup to mount them into the saddle.[3]

The Tories formed over half the Opposition, and without their vote Walpole could not be brought down. Leading Whigs in Opposition at this time despaired of ever being able to encompass it.[4] Blaming the conduct of some of these Whigs for the defection of the Tories, Dodington, a follower of Argyll, criticised—

> that foolish manner of discourse . . . which is, that we are such immaculate Whigs, that if any change should happen, we should be as sorry as the minister that a Tory should be employed, and would use all endeavours to keep any share of the administration out of their hands. How impudent is this! What man, or body of men, will act with another, to be made professedly the scaffolding of his fortune, and then swept away with the rest of the rubbish?[5]

At constituency level, Whigs and Tories co-operated together at the general election of 1741 which left Walpole with a majority of only

---

[1] N. C. Hunt, *Two Early Political Associations.* For the Church in danger debate under Anne, see G. Holmes, *The Trial of Dr. Sacheverell.*

[2] *HC* ii 111, 423; Stuart mss. 232/13.

[3] *HMC Egmont diary* iii 192.

[4] *Lyttelton Memoirs* i 178–93.

[5] Coxe, *Sir Robert Walpole* iii 573–4.

16. This made concerted tactics in Parliament all the more essential. In retrospect, it would appear that the section of the Whig opposition led by Argyll, Chesterfield and Cobham were either ready to pay, or willing to appear ready to pay, the Tory price for bringing down Walpole: a restoration. In August 1741 Chesterfield set out for France, writing of Pulteney to Dodington 'the silly, half-witted, zealous Whigs consider him as the only support of Whiggism, and look upon us as running headlong into Bolingbroke and the Tories . . . if the Duke of Argyll sounds to battle, I will follow my leader.' In Paris he saw Bolingbroke, and then went on to Avignon to meet his kinsman, the Duke of Ormonde.[1] Walpole was alerted at once. It is difficult for us to realise the immense prestige Ormonde had retained with the Tories. Vilified by the Whigs for obeying as commander-in-chief the 'restraining orders' putting an end to hostilities with France before the Peace of Utrecht, he was regarded by fellow Tories as 'the best bred man of his age'.[2] In exile, he behaved with unfailing dignity before every reverse and kept aloof from the quarrels and recriminations to which the Jacobites were all too prone. The sequel of Chesterfield's visit to Ormonde, was a letter from James to his friends in England dated 16/27 September 1741 and sent through Col. Cecil:

I must earnestly recommend to all those with you who wish me well that they should pursue vigorous and unanimous measures in the next sessions of Parliament. They will probably have many occasions of greatly distressing the present Government and ministry, and will perhaps find some who will concur with them in that, though not out of good will to my cause, and even if the first proposers of measures which may tend to that end. In such cases I hope my friends will make no scruples in joining heartily with them for whatever their particular motives may be, anything that tends to the disadvantage of the present Government and to the bringing it into confusion cannot but be of advantage to my cause. Opportunities may offer during the next sessions, which if lost, may return no more, and besides the consequences that my friends showing a proper spirit may have at home, nothing certainly can more effectually encourage Cardinal Fleury to declare for us. Enfin, I take my friends' behaviour next session to be a matter of the greatest importance, and I doubt not but

[1] *Letters of Lord Chesterfield*, ed. B. Dobrée, ii 468–70; *HC* i 71.
[2] Dr William King, *Political and Literary Anecdotes* (1819 ed.) 9.

when they consider seriously what they owe both to themselves and to
me, they will not be wanting in anything that may contribute to our
common welfare, and indeed that of our country. I desire you will
communicate this letter or the contents of it to as many as you can
with safety and prudence.[1]

Walpole said he had proof that over one hundred copies of this letter
had been distributed, that it was procured by Chesterfield through
Ormonde, and that the loss of the crucial divisions leading to his fall
'was the effect of these summer negotiations'.[2] When the new Parliament met in December 1741, the Tories came up early, contrary to
their normal practice, and in their fullest numbers. A well-informed
ministerial supporter immediately noticed the change: 'Notwithstanding the personal candour that was shown upon the motion last
year, there is some cement that holds the Opposition together now,
stronger than I believe any consideration will be able to break
through.'[3] The Tories voted with the opposition Whigs in division
upon division until Walpole had to resign.

Early in 1742, just before Walpole's resignation, copies of a letter
from the Pretender dated 14/25 May 1741 was sent round to Tories
and opposition Whigs by the penny post. In this he referred to a
Declaration he had just signed:

It contains a general indemnity, without exception, for all that hath
passed against me and my family. A solemn engagement to maintain
the Church of England as by law established in all her rights,
privileges, possessions and immunities whatsoever. And as I am
utterly averse to all animosities and persecution on account of
religion, it also contains a promise to grant and allow a toleration to
all Protestant dissenters.

I also express in it an utter aversion to the suspending of the
Habeas Corpus Act, as well as to the loading of my subjects with
unnecessary taxes, or the raising of them in a manner burthensome
to them, and especially to the introducing of foreign excises, and all
such methods as may have hitherto been advised and pursued to
acquire arbitrary power at the expense of the liberty and property of
the subject. And besides there is a general article of my readiness to

[1] *HC* i 71; Stuart mss. 236/73; Add. 9224ff. 2–4.
[2] *HC* i 71; Ryder diary 4 Dec. 1741, Coxe, *Sir Robert Walpole* i. 687n.
[3] *HC* i 71.

settle all that may relate to the welfare and happiness of the nation both in civil and ecclesiastical matters by the sincere advice and concurrence of a free Parliament.

George Heathcote, Member for London and a leading opposition Whig, sent his copy to the Duke of Newcastle, the Secretary of State.[1] James Erskine, Member for Stirling Burghs, was the brother of the late Lord Mar who had led the '15. Erskine had been prominent in concerting the tactics of the Opposition since 1734 and was connected with Pulteney and Cobham as well as Gower while corresponding with the Pretender.[2] He discussed the contents of this letter with John Proby, Tory Member for Stamford and Gower's brother-in-law. Proby approved of it, but he criticised James's advisers, especially Col. Cecil, whom he called 'a foolish man', and James Murray, Lord Dunbar, Secretary of State in Rome. Erskine replied that if Proby would care to suggest 'the most proper persons among the Tories to take the direction of H.M.'s affairs in England' he would transmit his proposals. The Pretender had written to Erskine to desire he should assure his friends among the opposition Whigs that if 'they enter seriously and heartily into measures for bringing about my restoration . . . there is no reasonable demand they can make, either on behalf of themselves in particular, or of the country in general, that I shall not readily and cheerfully comply with'. Just before Walpole's fall, Erskine gave Pulteney a copy of the Pretender's letter of May 1741. At their next meeting, Pulteney returned it, saying: 'Take your papers, I do not love to have such papers!' Erskine then pointed out the dissatisfaction of the Tories, and how difficult it had been to hold the Opposition together, upon which 'Mr. Pulteney answered that he had done exceedingly well, but now he thanked God that they were out of the power of the Tories, for Sir Robert Walpole . . . had sent to them and agreed to resign his offices and leave them to form a ministry such as they found proper'.[3]

For over twenty-five years the Tory party had been kept together, with only a handful of defections, a remarkable enough feat since its leaders had no rewards to offer. Their main concern was to negotiate

---

[1] SP 36/60/131–6. I am obliged to Dame Lucy Sutherland for this reference.
[2] *HC* ii 14–17; *Marchmont Papers* ii 2–4, 18, 58, 128–9, 167.
[3] Stuart mss. 240/140; 242/112; *HC* ii 16.

from strength and make terms as a party and not allow their political opponents to split them. This was, of course, normal political behaviour, but it was denounced by those whose ends were checked by it as obstinacy and short-sightedness. The public demands of the Tory party were: a reduction of the army, the organisation of an effective militia (in which they would be allowed to serve), a foreign policy based on the national interest, a repeal of the Septennial Act, the Riot Act, the Waltham Black Act and the Smuggling Act.[1] In other words they wanted all the repressive legislation passed since 1715 swept away. These demands were expressed in many instructions sent to Tory Members from all parts of England and Wales, and one was sent from Scotland to James Erskine. Those sent to Sir Watkin Williams Wynn from Denbighshire denounced 'standing armies in time of peace' who 'like the locusts of Egypt cover the face of the land, living in sloth and idleness, and devouring the labours of the industrious'. These instructions also demanded bills to prevent corruption at elections and the 'villainous practices of returning officers', and vigorous inquiries into the corruption and mismanagements of the late administration.[2]

A non-Jacobite Tory noticed at this time that 'the body of the Tories are suddenly listed under a new general, the Duke of Argyll'.[3] At a meeting of the whole Opposition at the Fountain Tavern in the Strand on 12 February 1742, Argyll called for the formation of a Government based on the principle of 'the Broad Bottom, a cant word which corresponding equally with the personal figure of some of their leaders [Cotton] and the nature of their pretensions, was understood to imply a party united to force the Tories into the Administration'. Wynn was doing his utmost to secure for Argyll the post of commander-in-chief of the army—to act as the General Monck of a second Stuart restoration. On Argyll's refusal to accept this office unless his Tory friends were given places,

> Sir Watkin Williams Wynn, with a considerable number of other Parliament men, repaired to his Grace, and exposed to him that

[1] *The Conduct of the late and present ministry compared*, 1742, quoted in A. Foord, *His Majesty's Opposition*, 234. For the Black Act, see E. P. Thompson, *Whigs and Hunters*. For the effects of the Smuggling Act, see below Chapter 4.
[2] *Gentleman's Magazine* 1742, 216–17.
[3] *HC* i 612.

unless matters were in a further way of settlement, they should all break to pieces next Thursday, when the Parliament was to meet; that when the question about the army should come on, he and the rest were determined to oppose continuing the same number unless his Grace were at the head of it, and therefore they pressed him hard to accept his Majesty's offer to restore him to his posts.

The next day, Argyll and 'the chiefs of the Tory party . . . waited on the King whose rooms had not been seen from the beginning of the reign so crowded', when 'the King was surprised to see such a number of new faces, gentlemen and lords of great property and interest in their countries [i.e. counties], but expressed himself troubled that (as he had heard) some of them said they would come but that once'.[1] Ryder wrote that Argyll 'stands out, and insists he will come into no accommodation till some of his friends are brought in, and particularly that Lord Gower, Lord Bathurst, Sir Watkin Williams Wynn, and Sir John Hynde Cotton are provided for'. On 17 February, the day before Parliament met, it was agreed that Argyll should be restored to his former offices, that Cobham should have a regiment with the rank of field marshal, and that Bathurst, Chesterfield and Gower should be provided for as soon as suitable vacancies occurred. On 10 March, Argyll resigned because the King would not accept his nomination of Sir John Cotton and Barrymore's brother-in-law Lord Granard as lords of the Admiralty.[2] At another meeting of the Opposition at the Fountain Tavern the next day, Argyll declared that a few were engrossing to themselves 'the exclusive right of nomination', adding:

> The choice of those already preferred having fallen upon the Whigs, is an ill omen to the Tories. If these are not to be provided for, the happy effects of the coalition will be destroyed, and the odious distinction of party be revived. It is therefore highly necessary to continue closely united, and to persevere with the same vehemence as ever, till the Tories obtain justice, and the administration is founded upon the broad bottom of both parties.

Pulteney replied it must be the work of time 'to remove suspicions incalculated long and long credited, with regard to a denomination

[1] *HC* i 71–2; *HMC Egmont diary* iii 257–8.
[2] *HMC Egmont diary* iii 254–6, 257–8; *HC* i 52–3; Ryder diary 17 Feb. 1742.

of men, who have formerly been thought not heartily attached to the reigning family'.[1] Privately, Pulteney told Bishop Newton that the Tories would have had justice had it not been for their 'mad ideas'.[2] Bussy, the French envoy in London, who for reasons of his own was on the closest terms with the English ministers,[3] reported that Argyll and Chesterfield bitterly attacked Pulteney and Carteret for taking office to the exclusion of the Tories. Walpole feared above all that Carteret would agree to 'a Tory Parliament [i.e. a free Parliament] which must naturally end in the Pretender'. Pulteney was said to have waited on Frederick Prince of Wales, advising him he should insist on office for Bathurst, Gower, Lord Carlisle, Lord Westmorland, Cobham and Sir John Cotton. The real obstacle was George II's 'unconquerable aversion' for the Tories.[4] To try to satisfy the clamours of Tories and some of the opposition Whigs, particularly those in the City of London, Pulteney presented a bill in March to prevent false returns at elections and secured the passing of a watered-down place bill introduced by Sandys, but a bill sponsored by Thomas Carew, a Jacobite Tory, to prevent court pensioners from sitting in Parliament was thrown out in the Lords by a large majority.[5]

In the spring of 1742, most of the Tories, especially Carew and John Philipps, warmly supported a motion to send the army to Flanders, but opposed proposals to bring a corresponding number of troops over from Ireland, deriding the possibility of an invasion or a Jacobite insurrection.[6] A memorandum in the French Foreign Office commented that Carteret's policy of sending all available troops to the Continent was precisely what the Tory party had always wanted.[7]

In June 1742 the news broke out that the Duke of Argyll had given his brother, Lord Ilay, to hand over to the King, two letters he had received from the Pretender. At first, Argyll said he had them from Col. Cecil, which Horace Walpole thought unlikely since

[1] Lord Perceval, *Faction Detected*.
[2] Foord, 224.
[3] See below Chapter 4.
[4] Add. 33004f. 86; Ryder diary Feb. 1742.
[5] *HMC Egmont diary* iii 262.
[6] Owen 132–3.
[7] AEM & D Ang. 78ff. 5–9.

Argyll had not seen Cecil for two years. Then Argyll admitted that 'upon recollection he thought it right to say he had received those letters from Lord Barrymore'. The first, in the Pretender's own hand, was 'to thank Mr. Burnus [the Duke of Argyll] for his services and that he hopes he would answer *the assurances* given of him'. The second, a copy of a circular letter from the Pretender to his friends in England dated 25 April 1742 was as follows:

Though I am very impatient to hear from you, I cannot delay any longer expressing to you my satisfaction at the late behaviour of my friends in Parliament, and I take it as a great mark of their singular regard for what I wrote to you some months ago, because I am sensible that some of them were not entirely of opinion that Mr. Tench's [Sir R. Walpole's] removal would be for my interest: as affairs have fallen out that even proves more to my advantage than could have been well expected, which will I hope encourage my friends the more to pursue the most vigorous measures during the remainder of this session. Whatever step they take, or measures they may pursue which can any ways tend to the ease of the people and good of our country will always be encouraged and applauded by me, though I were to draw no personal advantage by it myself, but that is not like to be the case in the present circumstances, and it must surely appear now very visible to all impartial men, who will allow themselves to reflect, that my and my family's restoration is the only effectual remedy for the evils the nation groans under, but it cannot be expected that it should be brought about of a sudden. My friends late conduct does them honour, it shows the whole nation the greatness of their influence and what they are able to do. I should much encourage them to continue what they have begun till they have perfected the work they have at heart. It is not a single member being removed that will alone effect it, but a steady, vigorous and constant pursuit of all such measures as may effectually tend to the distressing the present government and whoever shall be the chief ministers and directors of it, to the overthrowing all entirely at last, as the only effectual means to provide for the welfare of the nation. Let therefore all other views and considerations give place to this great and single object, let no private jealousies and party animosities obstruct a perfect union amongst themselves or hinder them from going heartily with whoever has their country's interest at heart, and shall even add with cheerfulness and sincerity, let them think neither of me, nor my family, but in as much as we may be the instrument of relieving our country from its present oppression and restoring it to its former glory and happiness for I shall always be happy enough when I see my country so. It is the only thing in general I can express to you, it is you on the place that can only determine on particular measures according to the different circumstances of things and I desire you would communicate this to as many of our friends as you can with prudence and safety.[1]

James Erskine was indignant, writing of Argyll:

> His conduct to Lord Barrymore is condemned by all the earth. He has long lived in great friendship with that Lord, and professed great honour and respect for him as a man of sense and worth, and one of the best officers in Britain, and though his Lordship was several days within a few miles of his Grace's house after delivering the Chevalier's [the Pretender's] letter to him, and so he exposed his friend to be caught napping for a treasonable fact, though it could not have imputed anything against his Grace to have given his friend previous notice of the danger he was to bring him into.[2]

Carteret, not wishing it to be known that the Whig opposition, in part at least, had acted in concert with the Pretender, suppressed the Pretender's letter, so that 'nothing was done upon it'. Walpole's verdict on this was that Argyll 'was got into the Pretender's scheme but when Colonel Cecil sent him a letter from the Pretender he had not the courage to stand by his promise'. Barrymore left immediately for Ireland where he remained till the end of the year. As to Argyll, after this he lived 'retired, hardly seeing anybody, or speaking to the few admitted to him, but as one moped, indolent, dejected and broken-hearted' until his death in October 1743.[3]

During the summer recess, Cotton met Dodington to agree measures for a new opposition, which opened next session. In the debate on taking 16,000 Hanoverian troops into British pay on 10 December 1742, Carte reported:

> Sir Watkin Williams Wynn declared that England was made a mere province of Hanover, and when there were some for taking the words down, Sir J. H. Cotton got up, averred it to be so in fact, repeated and justified the words so that the House acquiesced . . . Sir John St.

[1] *HC* i 72; Add. 9129ff. 123–4; Stuart mss. 241/52.
[2] Stuart mss. 249/83.
[3] *HC* i 72, 114, 441; Stuart mss. 241/52; Ryder diary June 1742.

Aubyn . . . declared it to be his sentiment, that we lived under a Prince who being used to arbitrary power in his dominions abroad, was minded to establish it here, that all his measures were calculated for that end, and that of the Hanoverian troops in particular . . . This speech made him in a moment the darling toast of London.

Sir John Philipps (now a baronet) declared 'it is Hanover and Hanover only that seems now to be our care', giving detailed figures purporting to show that £392,697 were charged for the Hanoverian troops by the King as Elector, though they cost him only £100,000. Lord Gower and his friends also weighed in against the Hanoverians. The Tories made all the political capital they could out of the open preference George II showed to his Hanoverian officers and his tactlessness in wearing the yellow sash of Hanover at the battle of Dettingen in June 1743. Although George II had shown personal bravery in leading in person the army that defeated the French at that battle, the Opposition, led by Chesterfield and Cobham, turned the battle into a propaganda defeat. Even the Duke of Newcastle, riled because he and Pelham were having to support in Parliament 'Hanoverian' policies in Europe without being consulted, denounced 'German politics, German measures, and (what is near as bad as either) German manners' and thought that the Hanoverian troops would have to be sacrificed to popular clamour.[1]

[1] *HC* i 72; Owen 157, 183-7.

3

The Plans for a Restoration

The death in January 1743 at the age of 90 of Cardinal Fleury who had retained complete power until the end, changed the European situation. No first minister was appointed to succeed him and in theory Louis XV was to govern personally as Louis XIV had done. In fact his successors were the secretaries of state, 'the four kings of France' as Frederick the Great called them, who conducted business without consulting the great nobles on the council of state.[1] Their aims and policies were quite different from Fleury's, and since they play a central part in this story some account of them must be given. They were led by the one longest in office, Jean-Frédéric Phélypeaux, Comte de Maurepas, Secretary of State for the navy since 1723 and a member of one of the oldest ministerial families in France. In spite of Fleury's policy of strict retrenchment, by concentrating on quality rather than quantity, Maurepas had rebuilt an effective French navy from the ruins of that of Louis XIV. He was also the minister in charge of French trade and the colonies. Beneath the appearance of a court wit, with a formidable reputation as a writer of epigrams and lampoons, he was a hard-working and able minister.[2] The Comptroller General of the Finances, the next most influential member of the ministerial group, was Philibert Orry, Comte de Vignory, who had held this post since 1730. He had the reputation of a competent, honest minister, rather than a brilliant one, and was regarded as common sense personified. By economy and more efficient administration of existing taxes, helped by the long period of peace under Fleury, he had refilled the treasury left

[1] Frederick II, *Oeuvres Complètes*, Berlin 1790, ii 187; *Mémoires du Duc de Luynes* v 86; *Journal et Mémoires du Marquis d'Argenson*, ed. Rathéry, i 340–1.
[2] Lacour-Gayet, *La Marine militaire de la France sous Louis XV* 88; Luynes v 89; Add. 32747f. 292.

empty by the wars of Louis XIV.[1] The Secretary of State for War, Pierre de Voyer de Paulmy, Comte d'Argenson, came like Maurepas from a ministerial family. He was regarded as one of the most accomplished and handsome men of the age, not only a good minister, but a leader of the Enlightenment, a friend of Montesquieu and a patron of the Encyclopedists.[2] Last and least was Amelot de Chaillou, Secretary of State for Foreign Affairs since 1737. He had been treated as a clerk rather than a minister by Fleury, and now looked to Maurepas for guidance on all matters of importance.[3] These ministers had very much disapproved of but been powerless to prevent France's entry into the War of the Austrian Succession under pressure from the great court nobles, whose only career was the army and only means to fame and promotion the battlefield. Even Fleury could not withstand the torrent. A great league of German princes to vote for the Elector of Bavaria, the French candidate for Emperor, was negotiated by the Comte de Belle-Isle, nephew of Fouquet, Louis XIV's minister. He was assisted by Chavigny, who was against a restoration of the Stuarts ever since the failure of his friend Bolingbroke's plan in the thirties. The agreement of most German princes was won by the simple device of buying most of them, at enormous prices. George II as Elector of Hanover was cowed into signing a convention for the neutrality of Hanover in 1741, and even to promise to vote for the Elector of Bavaria and to try to stop English attacks on French shipping by the threat of a French invasion of his electorate. This was backed up by military operations against Austria, successful at first but ending in the disastrous retreat from Prague in which Belle-Isle lost most of his army.[4] These policies had cost France millions, brought her no real benefit and were now discredited. In the light of this situation, the ministers began to review favourably the plans for a restoration of the Stuarts submitted to Cardinal Fleury since 1740, to which the cardinal had given nothing but fair words. The reasons why this policy was adopted were spelled out only in 1745, but logically they should be

---

[1] Marion, *Histoire financière de la France depuis 1715* i 30, 162; Argenson iv 198–9.

[2] Balteau, *Dictionnaire de Biographie Française*; Luynes v 90.

[3] Balteau; Argenson iv 239–40; Luynes v 89–90.

[4] See M. Sautai, *Les Préliminaires de la Guerre de Succession d'Autriche*, and *Les Débuts de la Guerre de Succession d'Autriche*.

given at this stage. They were as follows. An alliance with England
had been regarded as beneficial for French trade since the days of
Charles II, and had been so since 1716. The partnership with the
House of Hanover had begun to break down in the late thirties,
and since the outbreak of the war against Spain France had
been engaged in hostilities with England as an auxiliary of Spain,
though not officially at war with her. A Stuart king would not inter-
vene in Continental affairs in the way the Electors of Hanover had
done. Austria, still regarded as the greatest enemy of France, would
be deprived of a valuable ally, Sardinia would have to make terms,
and Holland would be neutralised. The Anglo–Spanish war would
end. France had no territorial claims against England, and if she had
any views on English colonies they were not stated.[1]

It was in this situation that Francis, Lord Sempill, who had super-
seded Col. O'Brian as the Pretender's representative at the French
court, went to see Amelot in the spring of 1743 with a message from
the Duke of Beaufort, Lord Barrymore, Lord Orrery, Sir Watkin
Williams Wynn, Sir John Hynde Cotton and Sir Robert Abdy,
asking for French assistance for a restoration.[2] A member of one of
the oldest families in England, the 3rd Duke of Beaufort was one of
the four wealthiest men in England. His father, the second duke, had
been lord lieutenant of Hampshire and Gloucestershire under Queen
Anne, and had obtained places and favours of all kinds for his friends
and protégés.[3] The third duke had *nothing*. Sir Robert Abdy, 3rd Bt.,
member for Essex, was a large landowner and a friend of Cotton's.[4]
As Lord Sempill plays an important part in the origins of the '45,
something should be said of him. Murray of Broughton's portrait
of Sempill is an attempt, an all too successful attempt, at character
assassination. Sempill befriended Murray, praised him to James,
introduced him to the French ministers, in return for which Murray
(whose testimony when checked against the French sources shows
him to have been a liar) did all he could to discredit Sempill. The
son of a Scottish peer who was out in the '15 and whose forfeited
estates were granted to a Whig relation, Francis Sempill had been
employed in missions in England ever since the days of the Atterbury

[1] AEM & D. Ang. 78f. 212; Luynes v 343 and n.l.
[2] AEM & D. Ang. 82ff. 67–8.
[3] See 2nd Duke of Beaufort's letterbook at Badminton.
[4] *The Houblon Family* 40.

plot. The dowager Lady Sandwich, a Jacobite living in Paris, welcomed his appointment, writing to the Pretender 'his sagacity, penetration, and integrity are employed in Your Majesty's service with so much vigilance and prudence, that I cannot make a better wish than that all who have the honour to be employed in Your Majesty's affairs may be endowed with such qualities as he possesses'. His papers at the Quai d'Orsay and the French foreign archives show him to have had ready access to French ministers and to have been on good terms with influential people at the court of Versailles, as well as devoted to the Stuarts. James later wrote to Charles Edward that no one had as much influence over his friends in England as Sempill. Sempill's message fell on sympathetic ears, but he was told by Amelot that he and his colleagues would require more substantial proof of support in England.[1] Balhaldy, the secretary of the associated Scottish lords, who was a close friend of James Erskine and had probably come to know the Tory leaders through Erskine, went over to England in June 1743 to see what could be arranged. There, Cotton had made it an absolute precondition that Col. Cecil must be kept out, observing that—

the Government was not and could not be ignorant of Col. Cecil's correspondence with Your Majesty [the Pretender] and yet suffered it to go on, notwithstanding of which he did not judge Col. Cecil to be a traitor but a fool, concluding as Lord Barrymore and Lord Orrery had done that it was proper to keep him in temper in order to avoid the effects of his resentment.

This being agreed, they and those 'in the concert the City of London' undertook 'to procure all reasonable satisfaction to the King of France'.[2] They all refused to give pledges under their own hands—as the Immortal Seven had refused in 1688, signing their Invitation in cypher only—as being 'dangerous and useless'. Louis XV arranged to send James Butler, a kinsman of Ormonde, and his master of the horse (*premier écuyer de la grande écurie*) to England under the pretext of purchasing horses for the royal stables. Louis XV was passionately fond of horses, and Butler's knowledge

[1] Boyer, *Political State* xxv 394; AEM & D. Ang. 78f. 19; Browne ii 449. For Lady Sandwich, see Duke of Manchester, *Court and Society from Elizabeth to Anne*; Stuart mss. 283/1.

[2] AEM & D Ang. 75f. 196; 82ff. 62-9; *HC* i 585 and App. p. 114.

4

of horseflesh had made him something of a favourite at court. He had been several times to England before on similar errands, so that his presence would not arouse the suspicions of the English Government. He spoke English fluently, which would avoid the danger of misunderstandings. Louis XV briefed him personally before he left Versailles, telling him to assure the Tory leaders that all their demands would be met 'provided he (Butler) was enabled to vouch for what was affirmed'.[1]

Butler arrived in London in the first fortnight in August. He was entertained by twenty to thirty members of the corporation, and had private talks with Robert Willimot, the lord mayor and Member for London until 1741; Robert Westley, the alderman next in the chair, who would be lord mayor when the attempt was made; and with four aldermen: Heathcote, Gibbon, Benn and Lambert.[2] George Heathcote, a radical Whig, had been sent the Pretender's letter of 25 May 1741 after the fall of Walpole and had then sent it to Newcastle. He 'opened himself' to Sir John Cotton at this time and thereafter became one of the most zealous Jacobites in England. He was an important gain, not only as an effective speaker in Parliament, but as one of the most influential men in the City. Edward Gibbon, Member for Southampton, the historian's father, was the son of a successful merchant, army contractor under William, who, the historian wrote 'would have contracted with more pleasure, though not, perhaps at a cheaper rate, for the service of King James', and had had considerable losses in the South Sea Bubble. Alderman Gibbon had been brought up in a household where 'in the daily devotions to the family the name of the King, for whom they prayed, was prudently omitted', and by a nonjuring tutor. Going on to Westminster and Cambridge, he was a scholar and a gentlemen, not a merchant, and soon found the duties of an alderman irksome. William Benn, who was known to have been an active Jacobite, was a member of the powerful city lands committee of the corporation, which controlled a good deal of its patronage. Daniel Lambert, Member for London, a Portugal merchant, had been very active in the agitation for war against Spain.[3] They were reported to have

[1] AEM & D. Ang. 77ff. 44–5; 76f. 209; 82ff. 62–92; Stuart mss. 250/169; 251/127; 252/40; 253/154. For Butler, see Luynes v 421.

[2] AEM & D. Ang. 85f. 82.

[3] AEM & D. Ang. 82ff. 71–2; 77f. 46; *HC* ii 121, 546; Beaven, *Aldermen of*

shown 'great zeal for a revolution'. A list of the corporation of London (in a hand not identified) was given to Butler, dividing it into Jacobite Patriots, Patriots, Hanoverian Whigs and Whigs, which gave 176 Jacobite Patriots out of 236 members of the common council (see Appendix II). According to the unknown author of this list, the City was said to have chosen—

> the most zealous and distinguished Patriots, governors of their public hospitals, and its advisers in affairs of moment, to wit Sir John Hynde Cotton, Sir Watkin Williams Wynn, the Earl of Lichfield, Sir William Carew, Sir John St. Aubyn, Sir Robert Abdy, Mr. Bramston, and others of the same kidney.

Butler was also told that the bitter opposition to the Court shown by the Independent Electors of the City of Westminster, an organisation which had wrested control of Westminster from the Court in 1741, stemmed from 'their attachment to their rightful King'. Later, John Sample, one of Walpole's spies, told Newcastle that most of the plans for the French invasion had been concerted with Sir Watkin Williams Wynn and Sir William Carew under cover of the meetings of the Independent Electors.[1]

Butler left London on 6 September for the Lichfield races, where he was met by Sir Watkin Williams Wynn and 'most of our friends', who expressed 'great joy' at being informed that Charles Edward would lead the proposed expedition.[2] Though nothing was put in writing, it was implicit in all the arrangements made that James would resign the Crown to Charles Edward, and according to a well-informed source in France, it had been made a precondition for French assistance.[3] The Lichfield races were a gathering of Tory gentlemen, usually presided over by Lord Gower and Sir Watkin Williams Wynn.[4] We do not know whom Butler met privately there, for he never wrote a report, and what we know of his

---

London i 195; ii 127, 129, 197; SP 36/60/131–6; Gibbon, *Memoirs of My Life*, ed. Bonnard, 12–8; Ryder diary 28 Jan. 1746.

[1] AEM & D. Ang. 76f. 202; Stuart mss. 254/154; *HC* i 286; SP 36/63/102. For John Sample, see Fritz 116, 121–2, 141–2.

[2] AEM & D. Ang. 86f. 214.

[3] *Journal et Mémoires de Barbier*, ed. Villegille, ii 385–6.

[4] Anne J. Kettle, 'The Lichfield Races', *Lichfield and S. Staffs. Arch and Historic Society* vi 39–44 (*ex. inf.* Dr Linda Colley).

mission comes from Sempill's papers, Balhaldy's letters to the
Pretender and a memorandum drawn up for the French ministers
by a clerk of the French Foreign Office. According to these Butler
met a good many 'honest' (i.e. Jacobite) gentlemen, who drank
King James's health, presumably over the water. Butler left Lichfield on 16 September, went to 'meet some friends in the neighbour-
hood of London' towards the end of the month, and did not see Sir
John Cotton and Sir Robert Abdy, who had been in the country
all the while until the beginning of October, and it is presumably
because of this that Murray of Broughton (who knew of Butler's
mission at second-hand through Lord Traquair, as representative
of the lords of the Scottish association) wrote that Cotton was 'shy'
at first more from 'timorousness than want of inclination'.[1]

The actual military plans agreed upon were not communicated
in full to the Pretender or to the Duke of Ormonde, because they
were thought to have been surrounded by spies of the British
Government. For this reason, there is more information about them
in the French archives than in the Stuart manuscripts. These pre-
cautions were necessary. In the Pretender's case, besides the agents
already known to historians, there was another and much more
dangerous one: an ecclesiastic called Rota, who was in charge of
cyphers at the Papal Court, and professed the greatest attachment
to James while he was in the pay of the English Government.[2]
Beaufort, Orrery, Wynn, Barrymore, Cotton and Abdy asked for
10,000 French troops and arms for 10,000. This was not to be like
the '15, a rising of amateurs against professional troops. It was to be,
as in 1688, an invasion by a foreign army at the invitation of influential people in England, who pledged themselves to join as soon as
the troops had successfully landed. The people for whom the ten
thousand arms were asked were not tenants of the country gentlemen, but the officers on half pay and the soldiers who had been
broke, who, it was thought, would join. The most essential part, the
French were told, was to secure London as soon as possible as the
centre of the government and most of the financial resources of
the country. Maldon near Colchester in Essex was chosen for the
landing because London could be reached from there without
crossing the Thames, because there were said to be many Jacobites

[1] AEM & D. Ang. 86ff. 214–15; Stuart mss. 353/154; *HC* i 585.
[2] For Rota, see Add. 32751f. 179; 32776ff. 73, 410–12.

in Essex, and because the English fleet did not patrol that coast. The Tory leaders asked for Maurice of Saxony, the natural son of Augustus II, Elector of Saxony and King of Poland, to command the French army, not only because he was regarded as the best general in the French service, but because he was a Protestant and was known personally to most of them. In order to conciliate the Scots, a separate French expedition to Scotland was requested under the command of Lord Marischal (the Earl Marshal of Scotland, who had been in exile since the '15). Absolute secrecy being vital to the success of the enterprise, the plans were made known to only a handful of people.[1] Apart from the six already mentioned, the secret was communicated to Sir John St. Aubyn, 3rd Bt., Member for Cornwall, owner of St. Michael's Mount and of large tin mines, who had been one of the leaders of the Atterbury plot in 1722 and had told Carte in 1739 that he could raise the tinners for the Pretender's service; Sir William Carew, 5th Bt., Wynn's friend, Member for Cornwall and a large landowner there; Sir Henry Slingsby, 5th Bt., Member for Knaresborough in Yorkshire; and John Baptist Caryll, Baron Caryll in the Jacobite peerage, the grandson of Pope's friend John Caryll, and the owner of Ladyholt and other substantial estates, but ones much encumbered with debts. He was the only Roman Catholic involved. Because of the landing place chosen, another five were let into the secret: Charles Gray, Member for Colchester, a successful lawyer who had acquired substantial estates by marriage, a scholar and a reformer who had brought proceedings for corruption against the corporation of Colchester of which his Whig father was a member, which had led to its dissolution and to his father disinheriting him; Samuel Savill, also Tory Member for Colchester; Thomas Bramston, Member for Essex, one of the ablest of the parliamentary lawyers, who had secured the passing of an Act of Parliament in 1732 to impose a £100 p.a. property qualification on justices of the peace in an attempt to prevent the inclusion of landless justices in Tory counties in order to secure a Whig majority; Mr. Read, who was described as a gentleman of great property in the country of Essex, probably Henry Read of Earl's Fee in Barstable, Essex; and Sir Edward Smith, 3rd Bt., of Hill Hall in Theydon Mount,

[1] AEM & D. Ang. 82ff. 65–95; 76ff. 186–7.

Essex.[1] The Duke of Bedford, through his father-in-law Lord Gower, was said to have given assurances of support for a restoration at this time, though Bedford was not to be 'trusted with anything before execution'. Gower had just been elected president of the Loyal Brotherhood, the Tory club (or board as it was called), in succession to the 2nd Earl of Lichfield, an office which by this time was considered tantamount to being the head of the Tory party. Like Lord Bathurst, Gower had not been active in the Pretender's affairs since the days of Lord Cornbury's negotiations, but he had presumably met Butler at Lichfield, and was regarded as committed at this time, which helps to explain subsequent Tory resentment against Gower and Bedford.[2]

Butler was given a list of the nobility and gentry in English counties and in Wales 'who could be relied upon' (Appendix I). Published in extracts (in a not invariably accurate translation) from a copy sent to the Pretender by Balhaldy and wrongly attributed to Butler, the list has been treated heretofore as showing men pledged to *rise* in 1745.[3] Drawn up in England, the list (in a hand that has not been identified) is now printed exactly as it was given to Butler. It was meant to convey 'the general inclination of the nation' and included people who were expected to 'rally to their legitimate sovereign' by 'declaring' for a restoration by way of a free Parliament, as had been done in 1660.[4] It was in fact the equivalent of the lists drawn up by Danby before the Revolution of 1688 of 'the names of the men of real position and influence throughout the country who might be expected to countenance a movement against James' in the event of a successful invasion by William.[5] Only those in the concert were expected to ride out to meet Charles Edward when the landing took place, and it was recognised on both sides that the advantage would be not only secrecy, but the fact that if the attempt failed, it would look like an unsuccessful French invasion, and no one in England would be implicated. Obviously the amount of support expected was probably much magnified in order to

[1] *HC* i 81–2, 529; ii 401–2, 425; *Quarterly Review* cxxxix 367–95; Howard Erskine-Hill, *The Social Milieu of Alexander Pope* 81, 83, 101–2; Morant, *Essex* i 259.
[2] Stuart mss. 242/40; Add. 32804ff. 286–7; *HC* ii 431; see below Chapter 7.
[3] Eardley-Simpson, *Derby and the Forty Five*, App. pp. 235–61.
[4] AEM & D. Ang. 85f. 92.
[5] A. Browning, *Thomas Osborne, Earl of Danby* iii 152–3, 157–63.

persuade the French. In sending a copy of the lists to the Pretender, Balhaldy wrote, 'as to the list of nobility there cannot well be many more depended on than those who are named there; and that in the state of the counties, it was not possible to make them fuller or distincter in the time or the season of the year, when every creature was in the country'.[1] It was a list of people expected to declare for a restoration provided a successful landing had been effected by French troops with Charles Edward at their head, conditions which were never fulfilled. Nevertheless, an attempt has been made not only to identify all the persons on this list, but also to define, wherever possible, the line they took in the different circumstances of the '45. It is interesting to see that most of the Whigs on this list were connected with Cobham, Bedford or Chesterfield.

How widespread was the wish for a restoration at this time is not a question that, on the face of it, can ever be answered. For the Tories it did seem indeed the only means left of ending a proscription which had now lasted twenty-eight years. Balhaldy at this time defines the problem of counting heads as far as Jacobites were concerned:

> The many sanguinary penal laws since the Revolution, whereby the crime of Jacobitism is rendered more horribly dreadful in its consequences than murder, witchcraft or even open deism or atheism … has brought such a habit and spirit of dissimulation on them, that a Jacobite can never be discovered by his words. It must be his actions that decypher him.[2]

Sir Lewis Namier noticed long ago that Tory family papers are non-existent for the reigns of the first two Georges.[3] Many would have been destroyed through the accidents of time, but in collections where they have survived before 1715 and after 1760, it seems a reasonable assumption to think there was something to hide. A nineteenth-century antiquary who had seen many such collections concluded that it was 'the custom in Jacobite days to destroy all letters with any hint of political or religious feeling in them'.[4] It ought to be easier to identify the non-Jacobite Tories, since declaring

[1] Stuart mss. 253/154.
[2] Stuart mss. 253/154.
[3] *Crossroads of Power*, 35.
[4] J. Robinson, *The Delaval Papers*, 56.

one's loyalty to the Crown was not fraught with danger and was indeed much encouraged by the Government; yet in the parliamentary Tory party, after every effort was made to find them, they turned out to be a small proportion of the whole. Some historians have regarded the bulk of the Tories as overwhelmingly well-affected to the House of Hanover.[1] If they were, why did they not say so? After all, the Tories were forward enough in expressing their loyalty to Queen Anne or George III. Popular Jacobitism is almost virgin territory,[2] but again almost impossible to explore after the passing of the Riot Act. Jacobite demonstrations did take place at elections when the troops had to be drawn away from constituencies, in Westminster, Coventry, Chester and elsewhere, but it is difficult to say how representative they were.[3] Again the Jacobite riots among the Cornish tinners, the West Country clothiers, or the Newcastle keelmen, were most probably economic rather than political in origin.[4]

The other papers prepared by the Tory leaders in the concert in the late summer of 1743 was a proposed council of regency for Charles Edward to consist of 'the Duke of Beaufort, the Earl of Barrymore, the Earl of Orrery, Sir Watkin Williams Wynn, Sir John Hynde Cotton, Sir Robert Abdy, the Earl of Westmorland, and Lord Cobham'. Westmorland and Cobham were included 'because of their reputations and abilities, if they can be brought at first to his Majesty's standard which is not much questioned'. John Fane, 7th Earl of Westmorland, had been returned by his friend Lord Cobham as Whig Member of Parliament for Buckingham. In 1734, he had been deprived of his regiment, the Life Guards, for voting against the Government without being allowed to sell out, thus losing £6,500. His resentment had 'led him to imbibe' what Horace Walpole was pleased to call 'all the nonsensical tenets of the Jacobites', and with the zeal of a convert he became one of the most active of them all. Cobham, a dark horse in politics, was a man to be reckoned with as the patron of the Cobham cubs, some of the ablest young men in the Commons, men such as William

[1] Hill 192–3; Owen 214.

[2] See N. Rogers, 'Popular Protest in early Hanoverian London', *Past and Present* lxxxix (1978) 70–100.

[3] *HC* i 203–4, 285–7, 339–40.

[4] See Carte's memo of 1739, Stuart mss. 216/111.

Pitt, the Grenvilles and George Lyttelton, though it is not, of course, suggested they knew anything of his game. The Pretender complied, adding to the council the names of Chesterfield, Sir John St. Aubyn, Sir Henry Slingsby and the lord mayor of London (Westley).[1] A safe means of correspondence between the Tory leaders, the French Court, and Sempill, was assured through John Lefebure, foreign secretary to the Post Office, and a secret Jacobite. Lefebure, whose 'zeal, fidelity and services' were said to be well known to James and Charles Edward, was in charge of the secrets department of the Post Office where intercepted mail was opened. His letters to Sempill show that he not only revealed whose letters were being opened but that he suppressed information most damaging to individual Jacobites from 1740 onwards. He was assured that no changes would be made in the Post Office on a restoration without consulting him.[2] Butler was given, besides the lists of the corporation of London, the nobility and the well-affected in the counties, a list of the exact size and disposition of the forces then in England, obtained from a John Mill, clerk to the Paymaster of the Army, and a secret Jacobite like Lefebure, through whom he continued to send military intelligence. Mill's lists gave 10,683 troops in England, 3,500 of them near London, and 4,530 in Scotland.[3]

The Declaration of King James, signed by him on 23 December 1743, deserves some attention as it was drawn by the six in England, to be printed and distributed there when the landing took place. As it represents the points most likely to appeal to their supporters, it may be worth quoting at some length:

We have seen our people, for many years, groaning under the weight of most heavy taxes, and bearing many of the calamities of war, while the rest of Europe enjoyed all the blessings of peace. We have seen the treasures of the nation applied to satiate private avarice, and lavished for the support of German dominions, or for carrying on of ambitious views, always foreign and often contrary to the true interest of the nation. We have since seen the nation involved in wars, which have been, and are carried on without any advantage to Britain, and even to the manifest detriment and discouragement of its trade, and a great

---

[1] AEM & D. Ang. 76f. 206; Stuart mss. 254/104; 254/152; *HC* i 286.
[2] AEM & D. Ang. 86ff. 70–109; Stuart mss. 254/152. For Lefebure, see K. Ellis, *The Post Office in the Eighteenth Century* 65–7, 80.
[3] AEM & D. Ang. 75f. 201.

body of Hanoverians taken into the English pay and service, in a most extraordinary manner, and at a most expensive rate; nor could we behold without indignation, the preference and partiality shewn on all occasions to these foreigners, and the notorious affronts put on the British troops. We have beheld, with astonishment, an universal corruption and dissolution of manners, encouraged and countenanced by those, whose example and authority should have been employed to repress it, and a more than tacit connivance given to all irreligion and immorality. Bribery and corruption have been openly and universally practised, and no means neglected to seduce the great council of the nation, that it might be more effectually enslaved by those who ought to be the guardians of its liberty. The manufactures of England are visibly going to decay, trade has been neglected, and even discouraged, and the very honour of the nation made a sacrifice to the passions of those who govern it . . .

We see, with a sensible satisfaction, the eyes of the greatest part of our people opened, and their present deplorable situation, and that they are convinced they can find no relief but by restoring their natural born Prince, whose undoubted title will of course put an end to the many calamities they have suffered during the Usurpation; and our satisfaction would be complete, could we owe our mutual happiness to ourselves and subjects alone, without the assistance of any foreign power; but should we find it necessary to employ any such, let our good subjects be assured, it is only to protect ourselves and them against those shoals of foreign mercenaries, with which the Elector fills the kingdom whenever he thinks himself in danger; and therefore, to disperse all fears and jealousies from the hearts and minds of our subjects, and to convince them, as such as in us lies of the happiness they may enjoy under our Government, we have thought fit to unfold to them, in this solemn and public manner, the sincere sentiments of our royal and truly English heart.

The declaration went on to promise a general pardon; 'to call and assemble a free Parliament, wherein no corruption, nor undue influence of any kind whatsoever, shall be used to bias the votes of the electors, or the elected' and to govern only by its advice; to support and maintain the Church of England; and to allow a toleration to all Protestant dissenters, 'being utterly averse to all persecution and animosity on account of conscience and religion'. The manifesto of the Duke of Ormonde as commander-in-chief, also drawn up at this time and to be distributed on the landing with the declaration, stated that the existence of a large standing army, many of them foreigners maintained 'contrary to the constitution of the Kingdom' made it necessary to call on a contingent of regular troops rather than to rely on the people of England alone. It stressed that friendship between England and France 'for 200 years with few interruptions before the Revolution of 1688' had led to commercial prosperity, whereas continental land wars since had proved ruinous to the nation; that the King of France had no territorial ambitions in England, and that the disciplined troops under Count de Saxe, a Protestant, would be under his (Ormonde's) command, and would be withdrawn as soon as a restoration was achieved. Convocation, which had never been allowed to meet since the accession of the House of Hanover, would once again sit regularly, and 'unworthy' bishops would be removed which would restore the rest 'to the public esteem they formerly enjoyed'. Judges would no longer be chosen from among those 'who have prostituted their vote in the Commons for years at the dictates of the ministry'. The commissions of the peace would only be composed of men of substance, and gentlemen from the oldest families in the land would no longer have to sit on the bench with 'mean, inferior people'. Younger sons of Tory gentlemen would have preferment open to them once again. Country gentlemen would not be made to pay virtually all the taxes (the land tax) to support foreign interests they detest. The House of Stuart having no interests separate from those of England, a restoration would end all the ills of disputed succession, and lead to the repeal of the 'incredible number of penal laws imposed to preserve a foreign monarch' and which 'made free speech impossible in the land'. Ormonde was to pledge himself personally to secure the repeal of the Septennial Act, the passing of a rigorous place act and the maintenance of a free Parliament with no government interference in elections. English officers placed on half pay and others deprived of their commissions because of their convictions would be fully compensated.[1]

There was an alarm before Butler's return to France in mid-October that Carte, who knew Butler, might have learnt the real purpose of his visit and talked too much, but it proved groundless.[2]

---

[1] AEM & D. Ang. 76ff. 235-7; 82ff. 32-38; 85ff. 97-8; Stuart mss. 254/92.
[2] Stuart mss. 254/152; G. H. Jones, *The Main Stream of Jacobitism* 222, thinks that Carte learnt of the invasion plans, but there is no evidence for this in the Stuart papers and they were not betrayed by him.

At Versailles Butler had a long interview with Louis XV, who professed himself satisfied. Butler wrote to the Pretender: 'I discovered, during my stay in that kingdom, a very fair prospect of success.'[1] In November Amelot summoned Sempill to inform him officially that the King of France had decided to restore the Stuarts. In December Saxe went over to England to reconnoitre, as Walpole later discovered, and attempted to establish a correspondence of his own with the six, but Lefebure warned that Saxe's letters were being opened, and Lord Barrymore insisted that all communications must go through his cousin Dr Peter Barry, a London physician, living in Craven Street near the Strand by the method already settled.[2] James wrote to Ormonde on 23 December:

> I really cannot tell myself when this may be delivered to you, because you will receive it only at the time when all is ready for the execution of the enterprise. The King of France is resolved to undertake in my favour. His Majesty required so great and strict a secret in the affair, that I was not at liberty to mention any thing of it to you before. He will take care you should have all proper lights and instructions, and I have only time to tell you that the affair has concerted with people in England, and that your old friends have a great share in it; and I hope you yourself will be in a condition to perform that great part which I have all along designed for you.[3]

While all this had been going on, the difficulties of the English Government increased. Carteret, who pursued a pro-Hanoverian foreign policy, had the ear of the King but little following in the House of Commons, while Newcastle and Pelham who commanded a majority in the House, were not consulted by the King. Carteret, in search of followers, was making overtures to the Tories, but they would have nothing to do with him. Pelham wanted to retain Gower as Privy Seal despite his continued Toryism and his opposition to the Hanoverian troops and to gain Cobham, who had closely associated with Gower. Newcastle wrote to Walpole, now Lord Orford, who was still being consulted behind the scenes:

The taking in the Cobham party and the Whigs in Opposition, with-

---

[1] AEM & D. Ang. 82ff. 91–5; 77ff. 42–3; Stuart mss. 250/189.
[2] AEM & D. Ang. 82f. 93; 76f. 42; 77f. 143; Ryder diary 26 Feb. 1744.
[3] Browne ii 450.

out a mixture of Tories, is absolutely impracticable, and therefore, the only question is, whether, in order to get the Cobham party, etc., you will bring in three or four Tories, at least, with them; for without that, they will not come.[1]

Orford was becoming concerned about Cobham's politics, writing to Pelham 'sure the Cobhams are not the authors or printers of the *Constitutional Journal*! That is such express and confessed Jacobitism that he must be gone as far as the late Duke of Argyll was if they are in that scheme.' Cobham's associate in promoting the *Constitutional Journal* was Chesterfield.[2] Gower insisted on 'the absolutely laying aside the thoughts of the Hanover troops' and the dismissal of Bath's (Pulteney's) friends, whereupon the negotiation collapsed and Gower and Cobham resigned. Horace Walpole's comment was:

All is distraction! no union in the Court: no certainty about the House of Commons: Lord Carteret making no friends, the King making enemies: Mr. Pelham in vain courting Pitt, etc. Pulteney unresolved. How will it end? No joy but in the Jacobites.[3]

---

[1] Owen, 167, 190, 193-4, 197; Coxe, *Pelham* i 94.
[2] Coxe, *Pelham* i 105; *Lyttelton Memoirs* i 217-18.
[3] Owen, 197.

4

The French Invasion

At the end of November 1743 preparations for the French expedition began, and in early December Louis XV informed his kinsman and ally Philip V of Spain that he was resolved to restore the Stuarts. France was prepared to meet all the requests of those in the concert in England with the exception of setting out a separate expedition to Scotland. Although amphibious operations are notoriously difficult, and were especially so in the eighteenth century when success depended on favourable winds and tides, the ministers concerned, Maurepas, Amelot and Orry set to work with enthusiasm and reported to the King without consulting the other members of the council of state. Despite his normally indolent temperament, Louis XV showed unaccustomed energy in issuing repeated orders and writing letter upon letter to say that everything must be done to make the expedition a success and that nothing must be allowed to delay its departure fixed for January 1744. Lord Barrymore, who pledged that all those in the concert would join the French as soon as they landed, suggested that they should come over in fishing boats—a kind of Dunkirk in reverse—to avoid attracting the attention of the English Government. The French thought that his plan would have been feasible in the summer but that they could not risk the pick of their army on fishing boats in the Channel in January without any protection from attack, and appear to have considered that their fleet, though smaller, was in better shape than Sir John Norris's at Spithead which, they believed, consisted of old ships manned by newly-pressed seamen.[1]

[1] AEM & D. Ang. 82ff. 80–8; 76ff. 209, 219; 85ff. 97–8; 86ff. 108–9; Marine B3/421/71–2; Colin 35, 36. As some documents are misdated by Colin and he does not give his sources, references have in every case been given to the originals as well as to Colin.

The Tory leaders were surprised at the scale of the French preparations, but expressed themselves delighted and agreed to send pilots who knew the Essex coast, a code of signals, and some persons of consideration to accompany the expedition one of whom should have naval experience. Suddenly, at the end of December Dr. Barry wrote to say that the six requested a postponement until after the debates on taking the Hanoverians into English pay. This was done at the insistence of Sir John Cotton, who said that if they left Parliament at that time the Government would become suspicious and 'upon the least alarm' would suspend the Habeas Corpus Act and arrest all their friends, whereas once the main business was over they could leave under the pretext of disgust at the Court getting their own way, adding that it would have the further advantage of the debates stirring public feeling against the House of Hanover. Lord Barrymore had been very much against this because the weather in February might be bad, telling Dr. Barry that some who might ride on horseback in fine weather would not turn out in the worst of the winter, that 'fat Sir John' might be one of them but that they would do without 'the effeminate and the lazy'.[1] The change did not suit the French who replied that though the concentration of troops along the coast might not attract attention since the Flanders campaign was over and they were in winter quarters, the Brest squadron was ready to sail and a large number of merchant vessels from the ports of Picardy, Normandy and Brittany had been taken to Dunkirk to transport the troops and ammunition under the pretext of setting out an expedition to America, but delay might enable the English Government to learn its true destination. Moreover, success depended on easterly winds, which are prevalent in the Channel in January, whereas in February westerlies blow more frequently which might prejudice the whole attempt. They had, however, no choice but to comply.[2] Whipped in by Wynn, Cotton and Philipps, the Tories voted in force in the division on the Hanoverians of 18 January 1744. In the Commons, they remained in the background in the debates, but in the Lords Westmorland and Lichfield supported Cobham, Bedford and Chesterfield in demanding that they be disbanded.[3] Meanwhile,

[1] AEM & D. Ang. 76ff. 219–20; 90f. 369.
[2] AEM & D. Ang. 82ff. 89–90; 91ff. 357–60.
[3] Owen 199; *Parl. Hist.* xiii 232–74.

Balhaldy had taken to Rome the drafts of the declarations drawn up in England and asked Charles Edward to leave immediately for France with as much secrecy as possible, travelling back separately. Leaving Rome under the pretext of a hunting party in the country, Charles Edward arrived in Antibes on 12/23 January 1744, but was held in quarantine for a week because there was plague in Rome. The delay enabled the English Government to learn of his presence in France, but it was thought he meant to serve on a French campaign in Flanders or that he was looking for a wife.[1] Against his arrival, the French struck 15,000 silver medals with the portrait of Charles Edward on the one side and the arms of the three kingdoms on the other to be distributed after the landing. A declaration was drawn up for Maurice of Saxony stating that the King of France had no territorial ambitions in England and had imposed no conditions on King James; that England and France had only differed because of the separate interests of the Elector of Hanover in Germany which were not those of England; that the French troops would be withdrawn just as soon as a restoration was effected; and that the ensuing friendship between England and France would bring commercial prosperity to both.[2] Military intelligence from England obtained from Mill and sent in a letter from Lefebure to Sempill stated there were now 11,550 officers and men in England and 2,800 in Scotland, giving their location and also details of the troops in Flanders and Ireland. Lefebure added that the greater part of London would welcome the Prince.[3] The French expedition consisted of 10,029: 334 officers and 9,695 soldiers, all French as the six in England had requested that no Irish regiment in the French service nor the newly-raised *Royal Ecossais* under Lord John Drummond should take part, since their mere presence on the coast would alert the English government at once. Balhaldy had gone over to England in early January to proceed with the final arrangements, and had meetings with Beaufort, Barrymore, Orrery, Cotton, Abdy, St. Aubyn,[4] Slingsby, Bramston and Sir

[1] AEM & D. Ang. 82ff. 80–92; Colin 28–9, 154–5; *H. Walpole Corresp.* xviii 378, 385.

[2] Barbier ii 385; AEM & D. Ang. 86f. 340.

[3] AEM & D. Ang. 86ff. 119–27; 90f. 323.

[4] Dr Linda Colley has suggested that Sir John St. Aubyn co-operated with the Admiralty at this time to repel the French invasion, citing letters (whose present

William Carew who expressed their zeal for success, but all refused a new request from the French to give pledges under their own hand. Balhaldy returned accompanied by Richard Barry, second son of Lord Barrymore, sent by his father as 'a pledge of fidelity worth more than the signatures the King of France had demanded and which they did not dare to give in case they fell into the hands of the English Government', and Lord Caryll, both of whom were to sail with the expedition. Obviously Caryll and Richard Barry had less to lose than the others in the concert, but, after all, those who came over with William of Orange in 1688 had nothing to lose but their debts. Barry was a lieutenant in the Royal Navy and his experience was relevant. He told the French that several naval officers would come over to Charles Edward, giving as their signal a white flame on their top mast. He named two as his and his father's friends, and commanders of two of the larger ships in the Downs.[1] The first was Christopher O'Brien, a relation of Lord Clare who commanded one of the Irish regiments in the French service. O'Brien had served in the English navy, then went into Russian service becoming an admiral in the Russian fleet, and returned to England in 1742 when he became captain of the *Princess Royal*, and commander of the *Royal Sovereign* the following year. The second was Hon. Fitzroy Lee, who had succeeded O'Brien as captain of the *Princess Royal* and was the uncle of the 3rd Earl of Lichfield. They asked that, in case of miscarriage, they should be given equivalent rank in the French navy. O'Brien, in fact, died at sea soon after giving these assurances.[2] Much less welcome to the French was the request for yet another change of plans. Instead of landing at Maldon as agreed, the French were asked to do what the Dutch

---

location she has discovered) from St. Aubyn to Borlase the Cornish antiquary. But this series of letters ranging from 19 April to 17 July 1744 (after any threat of a French invasion had disappeared) really concerns unsuccessful requests from the gentlemen of Cornwall to the lords of the Admiralty to obtain convoys for the tin ships and to protect the pilchard fisheries from foreign privateers.

[1] AEM & D. Ang. 76f. 44; 77ff. 140–1; 83ff. 163–4; Colin attributes to Sempill in 1743 a memorandum written by Carte in 1739, with no relevance to the French invasion.

[2] AEM & D. Ang. 82ff. 95–8; 76f. 44; 77ff. 140–1. For O'Brien and Lee see *Gentleman's Magazine* 1744, 53, 108; Charnock, *Biographia Navalis* iv 195.

had done in the Medway in 1667, that is sail up the Thames where Tilbury was defended only by a company of invalids, and to go as far as the Hope where they would be met by pilots familiar with those reaches of the Thames to guide them as far as Blackwall where those in the concert would join them. Blackwall was only two miles from London which would thus be taken by surprise. Those in the concert in London would foment a general insurrection in the capital. Pilots to guide the French as far as the Hope would be sent to France.[1]

Maurepas's plan was to send the Brest squadron out to sea with secret orders to be opened off Ushant. There, its commander, Roquefeuil, a veteran of La Hogue, was ordered to go and cruise off the Isle of Wight to prevent Sir John Norris from coming out of Spithead, but, if he could not, to draw him off towards the West and engage him in combat. While the Downs were left unprotected, five ships of the Brest squadron under Barrailh were to detach themselves from Roquefeuil and sail to Dunkirk to escort the troops to be embarked on merchant ships for the mouth of the Thames.[2] The instructions to Maurice of Saxony and to the French admirals said that Louis XV had decided no longer to recognise the Elector of Hanover as King of England and, at the request of persons of the highest distinction in England, had resolved to restore the legitimate King, James III. They were to act as auxiliaries to Prince Charles Edward as Regent of England. In the event of a civil war, enemies of King James were to be treated as enemies in war, but if King James's supporters were unable to maintain themselves, Maurice of Saxony was to return to France. The Comte d'Argenson, in a separate letter, thought it highly unlikely that persons who ran such risks would not do their utmost in the very sight of their Prince, and when given an opportunity which might occur but once.[3] On the *Dauphin Royal*, Barrailh's flagship, were to embark: Charles Edward, Maurice of Saxony, Richard Barry, Lord Caryll, Charles Radcliffe (brother of Lord Derwentwater executed after the '15), and Ormonde, who was not to be summoned until the very last

[1] AEM & D. Ang. 82ff. 96–8; 83ff. 179–80; 77ff. 85–6; 90f. 324; Colin 55–7, 65, 70–2 (Sempill's letter dated by Colin 29 February is 29 January).

[2] Colin 47, 55–74, 87–9; AEM & D. Ang. 77ff. 84–5, 113–14, 140–1; Guerre A1/3034/19.

[3] Guerre A1/3034/19, 55 and 82; AEM & D. Ang. 91ff. 264–5.

minute as all his movements were being watched in England. There were other Englishmen to embark. One was John Cotton of Steeple Gidding in Huntingdonshire, a nonjuror who had formerly lived in France after his escape from England as a Jacobite at the battle of Preston in 1715, and who had inherited in 1731 most of the Huntingdonshire estates of his uncle Sir John Cotton, 4th Bt. of Conington, Hunts. Member of Parliament for Huntingdonshire 1710–13. Another was a Mr Ashby, brother of Thomas Ashby, Member of Parliament for St. Albans 1734–43. The third was Read of Essex, one of the people at the talk with Butler in 1743, who was expected to bring over the pilots familiar with the reaches of the Thames.[1] An embargo was imposed on all English ships in the Channel ports under pretext of searching for contraband.[2]

In the first fortnight of February, the English Government had no inkling that England was about to be invaded. The Brest squadron was sighted at sea, but Henry Pelham, writing on 4 February, concluded 'they intend to intercept our ships coming in and going out . . . possibly to make us recall a part of Matthews's squadron [in the Mediterranean], or at least to prevent our sending any succour, or provisions', and thought it unlikely they were making for Ireland, as some people believed. However, he ordered Sir John Norris to go to Spithead to 'get his fleet ready as soon as he can', adding: 'I am much afraid we are not so forward in our marine here as we should be, however, I hope we shall be able to cope with this squadron.' As it was, Norris came out of Spithead two days before Roquefeuil was off the Isle of Wight.[3] At this stage, Newcastle was approached by '101' a secret agent with an offer that, in exchange for £2,000 in cash, he would give information of the highest importance to the English Government. 101 was the biggest catch in Walpole's intelligence service. François de Bussy, the illegitimate son of an impoverished noblewoman, had through her become secretary to the French ambassador at Vienna and then a senior clerk in the French Foreign Office. Greed and arrogance

---

[1] AEM & D. Ang. 75f. 201. *Gentleman's Magazine* 1731, 82; Stuart mss. 256/61–66; H. Broxap, *The Later Nonjurors* 310–11, 230.

[2] Guerre A1/3034/43.

[3] Chatsworth mss., Henry Pelham to the Duke of Devonshire, 4 Feb. 1744; Colin 154; *H. Walpole Corresp.* xviii 392–3; Add. 33,004ff. 59–61.

were his chief characteristics. He was recruited by Lord Waldegrave, the British ambassador in Paris, from whom he had borrowed money. One of the questions he was asked in 1735 was 'had France any intention of assisting the Pretender?' to which the reply was 'no'. In 1737 he was sent on a special mission to Sir Robert Walpole, as he spoke fluent English and Walpole bad French, receiving a special gratification of £1,000 from the minister's hands. Sent as envoy to London in 1740 he communicated the terms of the Franco-Spanish alliance to England and secret French orders to attack the English fleet in the West Indies. Ironically enough, it was Bussy who was sent to Hanover in 1741, where he reduced George II to tears for fear of an invasion of Hanover by a French army massed on its frontiers and bullied him into signing the convention for the neutrality of Hanover, a treaty he later disavowed under pressure from his English ministers when the threatening army was withdrawn. All the while 101 made increasingly heavy demands on his English paymasters. Newcastle paid the £2,000, and in return received a long coded message in which Bussy gave away the whole plan for the invasion of England, naming the Duke of Beaufort, Lord Barrymore, Sir Watkin Williams Wynn and 'Monsieur de Cotton' as the instigators. Newcastle asked if Sir John Hynde Cotton was meant or another of that name, to which Bussy replied that it was the Cotton who had escaped 'after the affair at Preston' in 1715, which Cotton was of course involved, but on the French side of the Channel. 101's message was decyphered on 14 February.[1] The very next day, the King sent a message to Parliament that he had received reliable information that a French invasion was preparing 'assisted by disaffected persons from this country'. After a debate lasting until seven at night 'not one (professed) Jacobite speaking', a loyal address was carried 287 to 123. The Opposition moved for an enquiry into the state of the navy, insisting upon a division in order, as some Government supporters thought, 'to show the French what numbers in the House they may depend upon'. Chesterfield moved the same amendment in the Lords, seconded by Westmorland, but the peers did not divide. Bedford's

[1] Add. 33,004ff. 22–3, 30–1. For Bussy, see my article in *History Today* April 1969, 273–6; Vaucher 311–12; C. Piccioni, *Les Premiers Commis des Affaires étrangères au xviie et xviiie siècles* 236–8; Sautai, *Les Débuts de la Guerre de la Succession d'Autriche* 300, 303, 497–8.

speech on this occasion, as Philip Yorke (Lord Chancellor Hard-wicke's son) noted in his diary, 'had the most Jacobite tendency of any speech that was ever pronounced in Parliament'. There were then about 10,000 troops in England Ryder wrote, of which only 7,000 could be assembled around London. Orders were sent for 6,000 Dutch to come over as well as 7,000 from Flanders and another 4,000 from Ireland. Sir John Norris was ordered to attack the French fleet, and if the French came near the mouth of the Thames or the Medway all lights were to be extinguished and buoys cut adrift. On 24 February an address for increasing the armed forces was opposed only by Admiral Vernon, an opposition Whig and a national hero since his taking Porto Bello 'with six ships' only in 1740, and he was seconded by his friend Sir John Philipps, three Tories including Daniel Lambert voting against. Philip Yorke commented:

It is observable that none of the leaders amongst the Tories, either on this occasion or on that of the King's first message, showed the least sign of zeal and affection to the government; on the contrary, they treated the whole affair from beginning to end with the utmost indifference and ridicule.

Yorke added:

The troops which were ordered up to London from different parts of the country, met with the kindest reception imaginable on their march . . . The Jacobites, to soften the unpopular sound of a French invasion and a Popish Pretender, began to spread it about, that the general who commanded was a Lutheran, and the young man himself is a firm convert to Protestantism, and that when his father re-proached him with having changed his religion, his reply was, he would not lose three kingdoms for a mass.[1]

The 1st Lord Egmont, another Whig, reported rumours that the Young Pretender 'is come only to relieve the English dominions from the oppression they lie under', adding: 'believe this who will: so said the Prince of Orange when he came in 1688, but nevertheless he accepted the Crown.' The Whigs, who had very good reasons

[1] *HC* i 73; SP 36/63/91; *H. Walpole Corresp.* xvii 399–400; *Parl. Hist.* xiii 643–5; *HMC Egmont diary* iii 285–6; Add. 35,337f. 47.

to be satisfied with the Hanoverian Succession, could not believe there was support for its overthrow among those who did not share in its blessings. Loyal addresses began to pour in. The London address, which George Heathcote had opposed, was presented by the lord mayor, Westley, and the two sheriffs, Lambert and Willimot, acting *ex officio*, as it was their function to present petitions and addresses from the corporation, and were knighted as was customary. Horatio Walpole was not impressed, writing 'notwithstanding the many zealous addresses, and particularly of this city, I don't wish to see a French army in England. Richard Cromwell was wont to point at an old trunk he had in his chamber of the lives and fortunes of the good people of England.' He thought there might well be 'a disposition in a great many to receive a new King, and an indifference in many more with respect to this family' and that 'the people may perhaps, look on, and cry "fight dog, fight bear", if they do no worse'. He was 'persuaded that the old leaven of the High Tories still exists' and that 'their principles in favour of the Pretender will appear as strong as ever upon the first occasion'. To Walpole, who watched every move, it was his life's nightmare come true. Bolingbroke, who was against any restoration of the Stuarts except on his own terms, wrote: 'The crisis is terrible—much to be feared—little to be hoped. God help us!'[1]

Arrests began very soon. Col. Cecil was taken on 24 February at his house in Masham Street and sent to the Tower on suspicion of high treason, and Thomas Carte was also seized; neither of them had had anything to do with the invasion. Lord Barrymore, 'the Pretender's general' as Horace Walpole called him, was woken up at 5 a.m. at his house in Henrietta Street, Cavendish Square, and was placed under house arrest with an officer always in his room and soldiers posted at his door. His house was ransacked to find evidence in his papers; messengers were sent to search Marbury, and Castlelyons was also examined on the orders of the lord lieutenant of Ireland for proof, but nothing was found. Examined by the Privy Council Barrymore said:

I have, my Lords, a very good estate in Ireland, and, on that, I believe

---

[1] *HMC Egmont diary* iii 284; *HC* ii 121–2; 196; 546–7; *HMC 14th Rep.* ix 92–3; Ryder diary 15 and 28 Feb. 1744; Chatsworth mss., Lord Hartington to Duke of Devonshire, 16 Feb. 1744; *Marchmont Papers* ii 327.

fifteen hundred acres of very bad land; now by G-d, I would not risk the loss of the poorest acre of them to defend the title of any king in Europe, provided—it was not my interest.

Egmont, one of the Whigs who thought there were few Jacobites left, had known Barrymore for years as a member of the Irish 'lobby' in Parliament and often visited him, but he was of opinion Barrymore was not a Jacobite! Dr John Beaufort, a London physician, was also arrested, apparently because he had been with Lord Barrymore, who was his patient, the day before. When questioned, he was reported to have stated that his only connection with the French was drinking a bottle of their best claret a day, and that he saw none but sick people. A list sent to Sempill of those arrested or questioned during the emergency gives the name of the Duke of Beaufort as well as that of Dr Beaufort. There is no indication in Government sources of the duke being arrested, but he may have been questioned. At any rate, though he was in the process of divorcing his duchess, he ceased to attend the House of Lords between 22 February and 15 March. Released in April on a £60,000 bail, Barrymore left London, and the Duke of Beaufort was later said to have done the same 'neither inclining to put their persons a second time in the hands of the Government'. John Mill, the clerk in the paymaster's office, was questioned after a servant of the Duke of Perth (who had been taken in Scotland) was followed to his house, but nothing against him was found, and he kept his place. Orders were sent to arrest Caryll, who naturally was not found in Sussex, but escaped further inquiries because he was thought to be hiding from his creditors. No one was charged or brought to trial. When on 28 February, the House of Commons was informed that Lord Barrymore, a Member, had been arrested on suspicion of treason, Wynn, Cotton and Philipps and 'some of the Tories' objected that he had been arrested before the suspension of the Habeas Corpus Act and before the House was notified, whereas in 1715 the House was asked for leave before any of its Members were taken, to which Pelham replied that it had then enabled some to escape.[1]

---

[1] *Gentleman's Magazine* 1744, 107, 165, 277; *H. Walpole Corresp.* xviii 408; *HMC 15th Rep. VII*, 328–9; *HC* i 73, 441; SP 36/63/102, 148–52, 154–5, 189, 197, 280, 282, 289, 373, 374; *HMC Egmont diary* iii 286, 289, 291, 293; AEM &

Not knowing what was happening in England, since Lefebure had forbidden Dr Barry to write as soon as the emergency began, Maurice of Saxony was awaiting the arrival of Read with the pilots and of Barrailh's ships in Dunkirk to escort him to England. On 15/26 February, he wrote to Argenson that he would already have landed in England if Barrailh had arrived instead of amusing himself by capturing English ships, and complained he had not seen anything of the English pilots promised, but that he was still pressing on 'since the wine is drawn, we must drink it'. The next day Barrailh turned up, but 'Monsieur Red', as the French invariably called Read, could not be found though searched for in all the Channel ports. It turned out that Read, who had volunteered for the task, had got to London from Essex on 16 February, the day after the King's message to Parliament on the threatened invasion and, in the circumstances, neither Barrymore nor Orrery thought that the secret of the expedition could be trusted to pilots, and that suitable people familiar with the mouth of the Thames could be found in the Channel ports, so that they sent Read alone. He arrived in France on 20 February/3 March, and, with little command of French could find neither Charles Edward nor Balhaldy, took fright, as Balhaldy later wrote, at the thought of the loss of 'his beef and pudding' and returned to England, leaving a letter for Saxe (not now extant) to say those in the concert in England asked the French to come over immediately.[1] As it was, there were available two captains of smuggling ships familiar with the Thames estuary: Thomas Harvey and Robert Fuller. There had long been a thriving illicit trade between England and France, smuggling wool out from the Kent, Sussex and Hampshire coasts to Dunkirk, Calais and Boulogne, and returning loaded with French brandy which was smuggled back in. The Smuggling Act of 1719 had only temporarily checked that trade, but it made the smugglers outlaws with 'nothing to look for from King George but a rope'. Traditionally, they carried the Jacobite agents to and from the Continent into England, and many were said to have taken the oaths to the King

---

D. Ang. 77ff. 206–7; 83ff. 189, 198; Northumberland mss. from Alnwick, Lady Hertford to Lord Beauchamp, 2 April 1744; Stuart mss. 260/108; *Parl. Hist.* xiii 669–70.

[1] AEM & D. Ang. 77ff. 129–31, 140–1, 194; AEM & D. Ang. 86f. 115; 83ff. 176–7, 179–80; Colin 105–8.

of France. At this time some of them near Rye were said to have publicly drunk the health of King James, success to Charles Edward's arms, and 'confusion to King George', without anyone daring to apprehend them. Harvey and Fuller, who were said to be zealous Jacobites like most of the smugglers, were held *incommunicado* but with orders to navy officials to treat them in the handsomest manner possible as they were married to Frenchwomen in Boulogne, and were very popular in that town, and any complaint from them might cause a riot there. At this point, secret orders were sent to Maurice of Saxony that if he was not met at the Hope not to proceed but to return to France. In fact, English pilots were already waiting at the Hope, and were later pressed into the English navy.[1] On 22 February/5 March, the embarkation began, and continued all next day, in the hope of coming over before any of the additional troops called for had arrived, and relying on Roquefeuil to hold Norris in check. On 24 February the Brest fleet lay at anchor off Dungeness with 15 ships of the line. Norris with 19 was anchored off Hythe within sight of them. Crowds of people began to gather on the hilltops to watch the expected naval battle. Then 'about three in the afternoon it began to rain', and this was followed by—

a dreadful storm of wind which put every ship in great disorder, and everybody in great consternation, some ships driving one way, and some another, and all in great danger of driving foul of each other. This storm lasted that night and all next day.

Eighteen of Norris's ships were damaged, five were put out of action and one, the *Prince Frederick*, was rammed and went down with all hands. Most of the ships out in the Downs sank. During the storm, Roquefeuil slipped anchor, and placing himself before the wind was able to return to Brest with several ships dismasted but no losses. The storms which blew straight into the harbour of Dunkirk and continued for several days more drove aground eleven of the

[1] 9 Geo. II Cap. 11; Stuart mss. 288/172; Edward Carson, *The Ancient and Rightful Customs* 96–7 (I am indebted to John Styles for this reference); Cal Winslow, 'Sussex Smugglers' in *Albion's Fatal Tree* 119–66; Add. 32,702f. 149; Marine B2/322/31; B3/421/51; Colin 102–5; AEM & D. Ang. 83ff. 189–90; 91f. 306; Colin 109–11.

smaller ships carrying the troops to the larger ships in the Road, and wrecked six of the latter. There was a loss of only a dozen lives, but the material damage was extensive. Six months' supplies of stores, provisions, tents and ammunition were destroyed, and the transports had lost their anchors, tackle and sloops.[1] Maurice of Saxony, who had been naturally irritated by two changes of plans dictated from England, was now in a flaming temper, writing to Argenson on 25 February/8 March that the men on board Barrailh's ships were more suitable to drive carts than to navigate; that Lord Caryll hesitated about everything; that Charles Edward looked for guidance to Richard Barry who was 'the innocent victim of his father's ideas'. He didn't know where Roquefeuil was and blamed James's friends in England for not letting him know that Norris was out in the Downs with the ships salvaged from the storms. He was impressed with the loyal address from the City of London, and showed so little understanding of conditions in England that, after expecting those in the concert to plan an invasion through letters sent by the English Post Office, he was surprised to find that none of them had 'taken off the mask' when arrests had begun and before the landing! He need not have worried, for there was no hope of getting across without running straight into Norris now, nor in repairing the transports or getting new supplies before the Dutch and other troops reached England. On 28 February/11 March he wrote to Charles Edward to say that the French government had decided to abandon the expedition for the time being.[2]

England made representations to France on the projected invasion, and on the Young Pretender being on French soil contrary to existing treaties. The French replied that since His Britannic Majesty did not honour the treaties he had signed, alluding to the convention for the neutrality of Hanover, His Most Christian Majesty saw no reason to keep faith with him, and declared war on England. From The Hague, the British envoy Robert Trevor wrote to his friend Horatio Walpole on 9/20 March:

[1] Chatsworth mss., Lord Hartington to Duke of Devonshire, 25 Feb. 1744; SP 36/63/142–52; *H. Walpole Corresp.* xviii 107; Colin 147–51; H. W. Richmond, *The Navy in the war of 1739–48* ii 82–84; *HMC Egmont diary* iii 288; Luynes v 370.

[2] Guerre A1/3034/91 and 113; AEM & D. Ang. 83f. 175; Colin 146–77.

The enterprise is certainly postponed for the present; but, as the French court has now discovered how sore and tender we are in this place, I do expect she will give us a *quietus* all this campaign; but keep holding the young man upon her fist.[1]

[1] AEM & D. Ang. 82ff. 106–10; Coxe, *Horatio, Lord Walpole.* ii 73–4.

5

A Time of Waiting

In the spring of 1744, despite the personal risks involved, Charles Edward sent Balhaldy to England to find out what was happening. Balhaldy reported on 11/22 May (given as decoded):

> The King's friends and Lord Barrymore's great apprehension is for the Channel, they cannot conceive by what means you propose to effect a landing while the Duke of Hanover is master of the Channel, otherwise they are as certain, as zealous and warm as ever . . . The King's friends [opinion] was then and is at present not to lose time but to come away as fast as you can with any considerable body of men. You will be in peaceable possession of England in a few days, for in a short time we shall be in a situation much wished by the King's friends. The Duke of Hanover goes abroad in about a week's time. The Dutch are to go back, five regiments more to be sent immediately to Flanders, so that you would have nobody remaining to oppose you, provided you are master of the Channel, or landed at the place you proposed, for Lord Barrymore thinks that the best place, because the Duke of Hanover's credit will be immediately blown up . . . There is nothing wanting but a standard, for God's sake let them have it, and it will be well attended. The suspension of the Habeas Corpus Act and the last penal law has exasperated the people, and to use Lord Barrymore's expression, it will be over shoes, over boots, once landed. When a landing was long expected the King's friends spoke to some of the leading aldermen particularly Heathcote, their answer was that you had nothing to do but to come. They are still in the same disposition and sentiment, so are the people of England (placemen and stockjobbers excepted) . . . The King's friends recommend in the strongest manner to have an embarkation for Scotland at the same time you intend an embarkation for England.[1]

[1] Stuart mss. 257/55.

The 'last penal law' was a bill introduced in April 1744 by Nicholas Fazakerley, a non-Jacobite Tory, to prohibit correspondence with the Pretender's sons, but he strongly opposed the clauses added by the Lords attainting the Pretender's sons if they attempted to land in England and instituting forfeiture of estates for such correspondence, describing them as 'one of the most pernicious and unconstitutional provisions ever devised'.[1] The Tory leaders attributed Barrymore's arrest to the old business of his having sent letters from the Pretender to Argyll, and blamed Col. Cecil for not having destroyed all his (Cecil's) papers, though nothing material had been found in them by the Government. The correspondence through Lefebure, which went through Holland, was restored with a change of cypher, and an additional means of contact with London was established through the smugglers.[2] In order to encourage the French to make a new attempt, from April to August batch upon batch of English pilots began to arrive in the French channel ports, though one group mutinied after finding out where they were sent! On 24 July Charles Edward wrote to Louis XV that he had just received an express from his friends in England saying that the kingdom was denuded of troops, and that another attempt could be made without exposing the country to all the calamities of a civil war.[3]

The political situation in France had, however, very much changed. The nobles in the council of state, led by the Duc de Noailles, Louis XV's Polonius, had been opposed to the expedition against England, and were offended at not being consulted. They advocated the more traditional ways of fighting Austria by way of a campaign in Flanders, and were warm partisans of an alliance with Frederick II of Prussia. This reflected the views of the majority of nobles at Versailles. In their endeavours to keep the secretaries of state 'in their place', they had a powerful ally in Louis XV's new mistress, the beautiful and haughty Madame de la Tournelle, who was made mistress of the Robes to Maria Leczinska, Louis XV's queen. When as Secretary of State for the King's Household, Maurepas was asked to draw up the patent making Mme de la Tournelle Duchesse de Châteauroux, he had diverted the whole court and

---

[1] *Parl. Hist.* xiii 982.

[2] Stuart mss. 257/91 and 95; SP 36/63/146; AEM & D. Ang. 77f. 219.

[3] AEM & D. Ang. 77ff. 234–5; Stuart mss. 258/71; 260/7.

much angered the lady by praising in extravagant terms her great services to *the Queen*. Amelot, who was dismissed in April, was made the scapegoat of the failure of the expedition against England, and the conduct of foreign policy was left to the council. The attention of the other ministers was directed to preparing the campaign in Flanders which the King had decided to lead in person. Everything was brought to a stop by his falling gravely ill and being on the point of death at Metz in August 1744.[1]

Charles Edward had been bitterly disappointed at the abandonment of the expedition against England, was tired of waiting, and humiliated at not being allowed by the French to appear in public. Most of all he feared that the failure of the expedition would be attributed to the ill-luck which had dogged his family for so long. He turned his sights to Scotland, hoping that Louis XV would let him have the Irish regiments and the *Royal Ecossais*, and writing to Sempill:

> I am certain there are many in Scotland willing to follow me though I would go naked and alone among them, and I will try my fortune that way, if I can do nothing better. You'll see by what I write to you how heavy the present disappointment is upon my mind, at the same time I inform you that no mortal will ever find me discouraged, while there remain any means untried.

He was encouraged in this by the Scots in exile who complained that Scotland had been 'neglected' since the French had not bothered to prepare a separate expedition for its relief, and particularly by Lord Marischal, who had been very offended by being summoned to Dunkirk in February and told to show himself in public, as he found out, only to act as a decoy to make the English government think the expedition was meant for Scotland should they learn of it.[2] In the summer Charles Edward received a visit from Murray of Broughton, the Jacobite agent in Scotland, who took the same line. Sempill introduced Murray to the French ministers, and Balhaldy, to whom Murray was said to be related,

---

[1] *Correspondance de Louis XV et du maréchal de Noailles* ii; *Mémoires du maréchal de Noailles* iii 357–8; AECP Allemagne 526f. 108; Add. 32804ff. 59–64; Duc de Broglie, *Histoire de la Politique extérieure de Louis XV* iii 440–1; iv 276; *Lettres de Madame de Tencin au Duc de Richelieu* (1790 ed.) 52, 56; Argenson iv 89.

[2] AEM & D. Ang. 91ff. 311–14; 81f. 93; 82ff. 105–6.

highly commended him to the Prince. In return, Murray, blaming them for everything which had gone wrong, succeeded in discrediting them with Charles Edward.[1] This had very unfortunate results. Sempill and Balhaldy both had a good understanding of English politics and knew the Tory leaders personally. Murray had neither. When he went to London in August (on his own showing) none of James's friends in England would receive him, and he was reduced to seeing only Col. Cecil and to blaming everyone else's management in his company. Consulted through Sempill and Dr Barry about the plan for a landing in Scotland alone, the English Tories expressed their satisfaction at the readiness of the Scots to rise, but they were absolutely opposed to an expedition to Scotland without a simultaneous landing near London. The reasons they gave were that if Charles Edward landed in Scotland, it would take him three or four months to get to London, and meanwhile the Elector of Hanover would have control of the army, the fleet, the public funds, and, as the Prince advanced, would be able to bring over not only English troops from Flanders, but also Dutch, Hanoverian and Hessian troops, while they, with no arms or military experience, would be helpless. Above all they wanted to avoid a civil war in London and the home counties which contained most of the riches of the kingdom. James very much agreed: 'I have been all along against an expedition to Scotland alone, or rather in general against any faint attempt the consequence of which might be more fatal to the cause than the not attempting anything at all'.[2] Murray always denied that he had advised the Prince to come to Scotland, even without any troops, but all the signs are that he did. One of the Scots who took part in the '45 wrote:

Murray had imposed upon the Prince and hurried him into it, without concerting anything with England. The English had always insisted upon a body of regular troops, not under seven and not above twelve thousand effective men . . . [as] under the Hanoverian government the people had been disarmed and overawed by armies of well disciplined troops.[3]

[1] AEM & D. Ang. 77ff. 248–9; *Murray of Broughton* 70–6; Stuart mss. 258/108; 259/199.

[2] AEM & D. Ang. 85ff. 131–3; 77ff. 248–52; 87f. 109.

[3] Maxwell of Kirkconnel, *Narrative of Charles Prince of Wales's expedition to Scotland in the year 1745* (Maitland Club, 1841) 77–8.

There was indeed a startling contrast in the situation of the Jacobites in Scotland and those in England. Because of the heretable (hereditary) jurisdictions, George II's authority just did not run in large parts of Scotland. The Scottish chiefs had feudal authority over the clans. In theory, the clans had been supposed to hand over their arms under the Disarming Act passed after the '15, but whereas the clans loyal to King George had done so, the Jacobite clans had kept theirs or only handed in old, rusty arms, and had been able to purchase and land others from abroad since. In Scotland there was no Tory party as such, and for over twenty years Argyll and his brother Ilay had governed Scotland by a series of bargains whereby they secured the Jacobite interest in elections in return for keeping forfeited estates in the same family. Nor could forfeited estates be sold on the open market. One man who had purchased a forfeited estate in Scotland after the '15 had his cattle stolen, his servants kidnapped and his house burnt down. Not surprisingly, would-be purchasers were difficult to find. The Scottish chiefs in exile still received income from their former estates. In order to govern Scotland, as the English Government found out in the '45, Argyll and Ilay had appointed crypto-Jacobites to places of trust, who either abetted or connived at the rebellion in 1745.[1] In England, the New Model Army had put an end to the chances of country gentlemen raising their tenants. Judging from the turnout at the royalists' risings during the Protectorate, even Sir George Booth's rising of 1659 which was supported by Presbyterians as well as Cavaliers, one would have had to conclude that there would have been little support for a restoration.[2] English country gentlemen were watched by government spies who reported any sign of dis-affection and were rewarded for doing so. The life expectations of a Fraser who defied Lord Lovat would have been short indeed, but by this time tenants of English squires would not always follow them in elections, let alone on a field of battle. Members of prominent English families who rose and were caught in the '15 in Lancashire, Cheshire and Northumberland lost their lives and their estates, and this decimated the numbers of supporters in those counties. English Tories were Jacobites in the sense that their

[1] Ewald, *Life of Charles Edward Stuart* i 123–4; *HC* i 159–60; Ryder diary 1 Jan. 1747.
[2] See D. Underdown, *Royalist Conspiracy*.

Sir John Hynde Cotton, 3rd Bt. (*c.* 1688–1752) Painting by Sir Godfrey Kneller, formerly at Madingley but present whereabouts (1978) unknown. By courtesy of the National Portrait Gallery

John Boyle, 5th Earl of Orrery, later 5th Earl of Cork (1707–62). Engraving by John Faber junior *ad vivum*, 1741. By courtesy of the Ashmolean Museum, Oxford

Sir Watkin Williams Wynn, 3rd Bt. (*c.* 1693–1749), and Henry Somerset, 3rd Duke of Beaufort (1707–1745), at Newmarket. Painting by John Wootton at Badminton. By kind permission of the Duke of Beaufort; photograph by courtesy of the Courtauld Institute of Art

James, Earl of Barrymore, an Ottway print. By courtesy of the Department of Prints and Engravings, British Museum

'A very Extraordinary Motion', on the Broadbottom Administration, December 1744. George II, leaning on a table, evacuates Lord Hobart, treasurer of the chamber, while the Duke of Newcastle and his brother Henry Pelham prepare to cram Sir John Hynde Cotton down the King's throat, exclaiming 'Push home he must goe down' and 'His Bottom's damn'd Broad'. King George cries out 'Hounsfool me no stomach him!' On the dresser several others (one of them George Lyttelton) lie ready to be forced down the King's throat, while two bystanders remark 'Remember The [treasonable] Healths' and 'Consider your Oaths'. On the left, one of the outgoing ministers shouts 'Damn their Broad Bottom'. By courtesy of the Department of Prints and Drawings of the British Museum (political satire no. 2613)

The '45 medal. Designed by Jacques Rottier de la Tour, goldsmith to Louis XV (*ex. inf.* M. J. Delaubre of the Administration des Monnaies et Médailles, Paris). The obverse is presumably taken from the 1744 medal (see p. 54) since a 4 is clearly visible underneath the 5 of 1745, with a different reverse. By courtesy of the National Portrait Gallery

'The March to Finchley' by William Hogarth. The guards marching towards the camp at Finchley to defend London in December 1745 (wrongly described in the engraving as the march towards Scotland). At the Tottenham Court turnpike in London, soldiers in very irregular array are going through to join the column marching away in the distance to the improvised camp at Finchley. On the right, the King's Head (a portrait of Charles II) is filled with prostitutes at the windows offering their services, with at the window under the sign an enormously fat woman, Mother Douglas, a notable procuress, praying for victory. In the crowd, young women are being indecently assaulted by the military. A pregnant woman clinging to a soldier carries in a basket a portrait of the Duke of Cumberland and a ballad of 'God save our Noble King', while another woman selling opposition newspapers grabs his arm. Behind the drummer, a Frenchman holds a letter directed 'A Monsier Monsier - a Londre' supposed to contain intelligence of a French invasion, and whispers the news into the ear of an Independent Elector of Westminster. Hogarth wished to dedicate the print to George II, who on seeing it exclaimed: 'I hate bainting and boetry too! Neither the one nor the other ever did any good! Does the mean fellow mean to laugh at my guards?' When told it was a burlesque, the King replied: 'What, a bainter burlesque a soldier? He deserves to be picketed for his insolence! Take his trumpery out of my sight', whereupon Hogarth dedicated it to Frederick the Great instead. By courtesy of the Department of Prints and Drawings of the British Museum (political satire no. 2639)

'A Sight of the Banging Bout at Litchfield', September 1747. On the right a
tent with the Hanoverian Horse is advertised to let. Heston Humphrey, an
attorney, is horsewhipping the Duke of Bedford, who exclaims 'don't you know
me?' The bystanders wearing clothes of plaid watch, as a fiddler plays 'The
King shall enjoy his own again' while trampling on 'God save ye King' and
'God save great George our—'. A peer (Lord Gower) says 'I was ye Staffordshire Jacobite'. Behind are horsemen in plaid dress, one of whom is reading
the 'Declaration of ye Hunters', while a man cries out 'No turn Coats'. On the
left, near a starting post, on which is perched a man in plaid waving a flag
with the Pretender's motto 'Pro patria mori' are two plaided horsemen, one
singing 'And a Hunting we will go go will', and the other 'The chiefest Harts
to slay'. A man on foot points to a race with one rider wearing plaid (Charles
Edward) and the other being very fat (the Duke of Cumberland), and shouts
'The H[anoverian] Prince five to one'. By courtesy of the Department of Prints
and Drawings of the British Museum (political satire no. 2863)

'Jaco-Independo-Rebello-Plaido', the Independent Electors of the City of Westminster, February 1747. The scene in front of Westminster Hall is the Westminster election of 1747 when Lord Gower's son, Lord Trentham, was returned
with Admiral Sir Peter Warren against two Tory candidates. One of the Tories,
Sir Thomas Clarges, was steward of the club of the Independent Electors that
year. The devil hovers over, exclaiming 'I have the Fee in my Hands'. On the
left, one of the government supporters cries out 'Give the Devil his Due',
i.e. the Jacobites. Crowds are rushing towards the house shouting 'no Indepen-
dency', 'no Pretender'. On the right the Jacobite house with a flag inscribed
'Morgan's ghost' and an owl saying 'We are all of a Feather'. By courtesy of
the Department of Prints and Drawings of the British Museum (political
satire no. 2856)

leaders, answering for the party, wanted a restoration of the Stuarts in the person of Charles Edward, hoping he would conform to the established church, but they had said again and again that only regular troops could bring it about. With scant regard for logistics, Whig historians have ridiculed them for showing their zeal to the Pretender only by drinking his health in secret. This was so, but after all, *in vino veritas!*

At Westminster, the struggle for power between Carteret, now Lord Granville, and the Pelhams had left everything at a standstill. Granville, who still had the favour of the King, had little following in Parliament, and in November 1744 offered the Tories *carte blanche* in return for their support, but, wrote Ryder, 'they absolutely refused to be concerned with him.' Pitt told Bolingbroke—

> that he had seen Lord Cobham, and had had much treaty with the Grenvilles, who were obliged to follow Lord Cobham, and that he saw the opposition designed to move questions, little, if at all, inferior to high treason; that the best method possible must be used to stop them, and to moderate, but that they must preserve the coalition.

Lord Chancellor Hardwicke thought that 'the body of the Tories' wanted the removal of Granville, but that their support 'can't be attained without bestowing, on some of them, honours, on others lucrative or honourable employments. But it may be attained without letting them into places of great power at Court or of considerable influence in the country'. They were still regarded by the King and most of his ministers as political untouchables who would prove Trojan horses in the Government, but had to be given something as part of a deal with Chesterfield and Cobham. They, on the other hand, wanted to make terms as a party and resist any moves to split them or pick them off in two or threes, leaving the rest helpless. Walpole understood this, telling Ryder the Tories 'would be hardly satisfied' with 'letting them into some places given to the discontented Whigs, leaving the old ones just as they were'. Gower was negotiating on behalf of the whole party, as head of the Loyal Brotherhood, the Tory board, and Chesterfield wrote to Newcastle on 1 December:

> when I had the honour of seeing your Grace last you seemed desirous to know the numbers and names of our necessary people in

6

consequence of which, Lord Cobham, Lord Gower and myself, have
prepared such a list which we are ready to give your Grace whenever
you please to command us.

The Broadbottom Administration formed in December 1744
included Lord Gower as Privy Seal, Sir John Hynde Cotton as
treasurer of the chamber, Sir John Philipps and John Pitt on the
board of trade—all places of little importance apart from Gower's.
Wynn was said to have refused a peerage as he was 'resolved to
live and die Sir Watkin'. Some Tory knights of the shire, it was
reported, were offered minor places 'by the mediation of Lord
Gower; but that serving for Jacobite counties they could not
hazard a new election, and therefore declined the acceptance of
them'.[1] Knights of the shire who became placemen usually did lose
their seats, as Sir William Pole had found out in Cornwall in 1712
and others since, but this did not mean the party as a whole did
not want office. As soon as he was in place, Sir John Cotton, who
took the salary but not the oaths, sent through Dr Barry an express
to the King of France renewing the pledge he had given, and
adding that the Tories in office would make sure even more troops
were sent from England to Flanders than last year. Lord Barrymore, at this time, wrote to Newcastle, who did not know that
Richard Barry had just returned from France, complaining that his
son had been passed over 'in the course of preferment' and that
'several have been made captains that were his juniors'. In fact
Newcastle obtained his promotion to the rank of commander.
Presumably George II, who reserved army appointments for himself, but did not concern himself with the navy, made no objections.
In January 1745 Wynn spoke and voted with the Government for
the first time in his life, in favour of sending the army to Flanders,
saying 'that he did not doubt that all his friends would do the same,
and that the whole nation would be unanimous in it'.[2]

Gower was regarded by the Tories as having taken office on terms
which amounted to unconditional surrender, and not meeting the
conditions agreed upon.[3] These were, on past form, a real end to

[1] Ryder diary Nov. and Dec. 1744; Owen 240–1; *Letters of Lord Chesterfield*
ii 541; *HC* i 544; Coxe, *Horatio, Lord Walpole* ii 106.
[2] AEM & D. Ang. 77ff. 49– 50; *HC* i 442; ii 543–5.
[3] Dr William King, *Anecdotes* 45–6.

the proscription, the repeal of the penal laws passed since 1715, stricter place and pension bills, the repeal of the Septennial Act and a free Parliament, measures which, if implemented, would have given them a majority in Parliament and the ability to do as they chose. Bolingbroke, who was infuriated at the failure of most of the party to toe the line, denounced the Tories as a set of men—

> who mean nothing, or who mean confusion. They are made to be 'hewers of wood, and drawers of water'. Such let them remain, since they seem to proscribe every administration alike, which is to proscribe government itself, even when the proscription, they have complained of so long, is taken off.

The proscription had, of course, not been effectively taken off, and the King refused to take in any more Tories. In fact Bolingbroke himself gained nothing from the formation of the Broadbottom he had worked so hard to bring about. He then suggested to Hardwicke a way out might be to put more Tories on the commissions of the peace.[1] This was not because they were more parochial in their outlook, and indeed remodelling the commissions had an often decisive effect on the elections as the Whigs had found in 1690, 1702 and 1710, but because it was regarded as the most harmless bait politically. Newcastle wrote to Chesterfield, who was then on a mission at The Hague, on 26 March 1745:

> The Duke of Beaufort has set himself up, and the Tories have taken him, for the head of their party: in consequence of which they have excluded Lord Gower from a negotiation depending about justices of the peace, put it into the hands of the Duke of Beaufort; and, upon an unsatisfactory answer, given to what really was no proposal, Sir Watkin Williams, Sir John Hynde Cotton, and one hundred and nine more, voted in our last question, about the £100,000, to be given for extraordinary services of the war, against 247, amongst which were all the Whigs, your friends, all Lord Gower's family, and upon the whole, near forty Tories. This affords the best opportunity to Lord Gower, so ill used by them, to separate and detach a number, which, with your Whigs and our old Corps, would form a body not to be resisted. . . . If you write to Lord Gower, for God's sake, preach up firmness towards those who have left him; and moderation and inclination towards those who desire to join with him.

[1] *Marchmont Papers* ii 340; Dickinson 286–7; Add. 32804f. 309; *Letters of Lord Chesterfield* ii 597.

Lord Noel Somerset had succeeded his brother as 4th Duke of Beaufort, and was one of the chief of the 'remitters', as those who sent money to the Pretender were called. Horace Walpole reported:

> The new Duke of Beaufort, a most determined and unwavering Jacobite, has openly set himself at the head of the party and forced them to vote against the Court and to remove Lord Gower. My wise cousin Sir John Philipps has resigned his place, and it is believed that Sir John Cotton will soon resign.

Chesterfield, answering Newcastle on 2/13 April, wrote:

> I don't much mind the Duke of Beaufort's opposition, which singly as his, and a few of the red hot absurd Tories, might rather do good than hurt; but then such reasonable satisfaction should be given to the others, as to enable Gower to carry off the best, and leave only a marked avowed Jacobite faction behind him. Little things, and in my mind prudent things in themselves, would I am convinced strip this new opposition of Watkin Williams, and Lord Oxford, the only two people to be regarded in it. Therefore for God's sake my dear Lord do all that is possible, nationally to satisfy the reasonable part of that party, and then you may with safety and even with advantage despize the rest . . . I will write to Gower, whose good intentions I know, but I know his distress too; and it is impossible for me to advise him to do, that which if I were in his place, I would not do myself. I would by no means have him intimidated by an unreasonable party clamour, and if he can make a decent schism of the Tory party, I would have him stand it, but if he cannot do that, I cannot advise him to stand single, a supposed apostate from a party of which he was once the head, and which will remain too numerous and possessed of too many national pretences at least, to be called Jacobite or factious.

To Gower, Chesterfield said:

> the small band of opposition which I find is forming itself under the Duke of Beaufort's banner, would I believe give neither of us much trouble were it not for two or three names that I see in that list, I mean Lord Oxford, Watkin and Cotton. I confess I am astonished at the first and the last. For I make allowances for Watkin's prejudices and Welsh popularity. But Lord Oxford's cool good sense and Cotton's sagacity, I thought would have hindered them both from engaging in a measure that must have the worst consequences, both

with regard to the public, and with regard to the Tory party in particular. I can more easily represent to myself your distress in this situation of your party, than point contrary means of redress of the evil. You little want, and I am less able to give advice. But I should think you ought to stand it out with firmness for some time at least, and with such of the Tories as will adhere to you, which I cannot think will be an insignificant number. And in the meantime work hard to recover Lord Oxford, Watkin, and Cotton, this last will in my mind be willing to be recovered. And Lord Oxford will surely recover himself; but in all events you cannot in my opinion yield to this attack which is directed in a manner personally at you, and be dragged through all the absurdities of such an ignorant hot headed set of people. If our friends in the Administration are wise they will contrive to strengthen your hands, by such concessions as will satisfy the reasonable and greater part of the Tories in the nation, and so brand the others with Jacobitism and faction.

Edward Harley, nephew of the first Lord Oxford, had succeeded as 3rd Earl of Oxford. As a Member of Parliament he had kept a valuable parliamentary diary, had been influential as the head of a Tory board or club to promote a bill to prevent the packing of juries and other reforms, the membership of which overlapped with the Tory Board, the Loyal Brotherhood. Recent research on Tory party organisation helps to explain the reasons for the survival of the party but it does not explain why they were outcasts. The 3rd Earl of Oxford has been said to have been 'unquestionably loyal to the Hanoverian dynasty' and a close friend of Philip Yorke, with no evidence given for these statements, and a search through contemporary sources has failed to reveal any. It is true that Oxford had not been a party to the negotiations with the French since 1743, but Carte who knew him describes him as being devoted to the Pretender's cause.[1] What in fact happened was that 'when it was discovered that Gower was really a friend to the Hanover succession, the Tories discarded him for being their leader, and adopted a determined Jacobite the Duke of Beaufort in his stead'.[2] In the hope of placating the Tories, the Pelhams and

[1] Lord Fitzmaurice, *Life of William, earl of Shelburne* i 49–50; Add. 32804ff. 287–8, 291–2; PRO Granville papers 30/29/1/11; Dr Linda Colley, *Historical Journal* xx (1977) 77–95; *HC* ii 111; Stuart mss. Box 1 /299.
[2] *Lyttelton Memoirs* i 238.

Hardwicke, who continued to deal with Gower, included more Tories in the Gloucestershire, Yorkshire, Bedfordshire, Lincolnshire, Hampshire, Cambridgeshire, and Oxfordshire commissions,[1] a process which was only stopped after the battle of Prestonpans. It proved of little assistance to Gower, who far from bringing over a hundred Tories carried only six, three of them his own relations: Baptist and William Leveson Gower, Lord Trentham, Thomas and Charles Gore, John Pitt and (temporarily) George Venables Vernon. He could not bring in John Proby nor Randle Wilbraham whom he had brought into Parliament at Newcastle. Dr King, who knew Gower well, commented that his defection—

> was a great blow to the Tory party, and a singular disappointment to all his friends. For no one had entertained the least jealousy or suspicion of this part of his conduct... The Tories considered him as their chief; they placed the greatest confidence in him, and did nothing without his advice and approbation. They even persuaded themselves that he had an excellent judgement and understanding, though his parts were very moderate, and his learning superficial.[2]

While all this was taking place, across the Channel letters from James's friends in England had suddenly stopped. This was done by Lefebure after two letters from Balhaldy to Dr Barry of 7 and 14 January 1745 had been intercepted by the Government and the names of Lord Barrymore and Sir Watkin Williams Wynn correctly decyphered. James wrote to Sempill:

> I am, with reason, very anxious as to what relates to the security of our correspondent of the Post Office, both on his own account, and because of the bad consequences it would be to be deprived of that channel of correspondence... The Government may have taken such steps and precautions as may give a just motive of jealousy to the person concerned, and make him think they know more than they really do.

It turned out there had been no treachery but an indiscretion on the part of the banker in Holland through whom the letters were sent; the venue was changed and contact was renewed in June.

[1] Add. 35,602ff. 46, 50, 54, 83.
[2] *Anecdotes* 45–8.

In that month Dr Barry sent a message from Wynn and Cotton, who led the Tories in the Commons, joined by Beaufort as the head of the party, to say that almost all the troops were out of England so that 'if the Prince lands in present circumstances with ten battalions or even smaller body of troops there will be no opposition'.[1] As it was 'impossible to get any stranger into England without arousing suspicion', they and their friends offered 'to open themselves' to the Maréchal comte de Belle-Isle, then a prisoner in Windsor Castle but one who was allowed a good deal of latitude there. This offer was not accepted because the French secretaries of state had no wish to give Belle-Isle an important role to play, and because Belle-Isle's wife, though a relation of Charles Edward through his mother, objected that he had given his word to the English Government that he would remain neutral in order to obtain the amount of freedom he enjoyed, and that he could not break it.[2] Instead of this, the Tory leaders sent to France Lord Orrery's cousin Robert Maccarty, 5th Earl of Clancarty [I], chosen because he was a naval officer with practical knowledge of the Essex coast, and also, it must be said, because he had not too much to lose. Clancarty's father had forfeited estates worth £90,000 a year by adhering to James II in Ireland, and had married a daughter of Sunderland. Regarded by Horace Walpole as 'of great parts, but mad and drunken', he had fought to recover his estates in co. Cork in a lawsuit at which the Duchess of Marlborough was 'said to be at the whole expense'. Failing in this, he was given a commission in the Navy, was made governor of Newfoundland in 1733–5, and was given a pension of £1,000 p.a. by the Government. What he wanted was to recover his estates. Arriving in France in August, he brought a message from Beaufort, Lichfield, Orrery, Barrymore, Wynn and Cotton, asking for 10,000 troops and 30,000 arms to be landed near Maldon and pledging themselves to meet them on landing. The 3rd Earl of Lichfield was the son of Gower's predecessor as the head of the Tory Board, and the brother of Hon. Fitzroy Lee, who had offered to join Charles Edward in the spring of 1744. Lichfield's sister and eventual

---

[1] SP 36/65/4 and 10; Browne ii 454, 456, 462; Stuart mss. 263/37 and 265/207.
[2] Stuart mss. 266/33; AEM & D. Ang. 78ff, 46–50. For Belle-Isle's imprisonment in England see SP 78/231; for Madame de Belle-Isle see *Mémoires de Saint-Simon*, ed. Boislisle, xv 154, xxxvi 70–2.

heir had just married Henry Dillon, 11th Viscount Dillon [I], the commander of an Irish regiment in the French service and himself a zealous Jacobite. Sitting in the Commons as Lord Quarendon, Lichfield has been regarded as 'the most promising in point of parts amongst all the young men of the Tory party'. Those still in the concert with them were Sir Henry Slingsby, Sir Robert Abdy, Thomas Bramston and Sir Edward Smith. Carew and St. Aubyn had died; Read had, not surprisingly, been dropped.[1] As it turned out, the moment was well chosen, for the conduct of foreign affairs by the nobles on the council of state had proved disastrous, Madame de Châteauroux was dead, and with the secretaries of state once more in full charge and the *rapprochement* between England and Prussia, French policy was again turning towards a restoration of the Stuarts. But Charles Edward, without consulting his friends in England, the French ministers or his father, had already landed in Scotland.

---

[1] AEM & D. Ang. 77ff. 126–7; 78ff. 46–50; *H. Walpole Corresp.* xix 160; *Orrery Papers* i 132, 190. For the Duchess of Marlborough and the Jacobites, see *HC* ii 66–7. Cokayne, *Complete Peerage* vii 647; AEM & D. Ang. 78ff. 46–50; 54f. 12.

England and the '45

If historians, Scottish historians particularly, have never left the '45 in Scotland alone, historians have left the '45 in England very strictly alone, or dismissed it as never a serious threat. The Scottish story is obviously the more attractive proposition: the story of David against Goliath, of Lochiel and other chiefs so moved by the youth and bravery of Charles Edward that they raised their clans contrary to their better judgment and, joining a handful of men, went on to win a kingdom. The English story is much more complex, with heroics conspicuously absent on both sides. It is proposed to examine the statements of Lord George Murray, Lord Elcho and Murray of Broughton, who seem to have expected the Tory gentlemen to raise their clans, that there was little support in England for the Stuarts, that Government forces had overwhelming superiority, and that there was no hope of assistance from France, and to let contemporaries, some of them nearest to the centre of power and to the seat of war, speak for themselves.

Charles Edward left St. Nazaire on 3/14 July on the *Doutelle*, a vessel belonging to Anthony Walshe, a shipowner of Irish extraction, landing at Moidart on 15 July. George II was in Hanover, pursuing ambitious diplomatic schemes in the Empire with Granville (who was out of office since the Broadbottom ministry) without consulting the Pelhams or Hardwicke, and England denuded of troops. It took several weeks for the Duke of Newcastle even to be able to discover that the Prince had already landed and that a substantial number of clans had joined him. Henry Pelham took a Walpolean view of the situation, sending at once for 6,000 Dutch troops, and writing to Argyll (the former Lord Ilay) as early as 20 August: 'I see the contagion spread in all parts . . . For my part, I have long dreaded it, and am as much convinced as my late friend Lord Orford was, that this country will be fought for some time before this year is over.' Granville and Lord Tweeddale, the Secretary of State for Scotland, advised the King that there was no cause for alarm. Although the Pelhams suspected Granville of acting the part of Sunderland to James II, it would seem that Granville regarded the rebellion as a tiresome interruption to his plans for a grand alliance on the Continent. Henry Pelham wrote to Chesterfield on 10 September:

> I heartily wish the troops were arrived both Dutch and English, for though I look upon these Highland rebels as a sort of rabble, yet if there is no force to oppose them, they may come in time to be considerable. We have scarce any regular troops in the country, and between you and I, I don't find that zeal to venture purses and lives that I formerly remember.

The Dutch landed by mid-September and were ordered to Lancashire. It took the total rout of Sir John Cope at Prestonpans on 21 September, which made the rebels masters of Scotland, to alarm George II, who had just returned from Hanover, and to make him agree to recall some of the troops from Flanders and Ireland and to send 8,000 troops under Marshal Wade to Northumberland. Lord Perceval, later 2nd Lord Egmont, a Whig, proposed to Pelham that the Hanoverians and the Hessians should be called over at once, but this was not done. Horatio Walpole told Ryder that 'if the rebels should make a progress, the King hated his son so much that he might be induced to composition with the Pretender, by giving up this Crown and saving Hanover'. Winnington, a Whig who was regarded as one of the ablest men in the Government and came from a Tory family, told Egmont 'he believed certainly the Pretender would succeed', and, until the retreat from Derby, continued to assert that the rebellion would succeed and there would be a restoration. On 28 September the Cabinet was concerned to find that a run on the Bank of England had begun and that the Bank having run out of other species was forced to pay in silver. The Government was unable to raise a loan in the City in the normal way as most people had ceased to pay the land tax. An association of London merchants 'saved the Bank for a time' when they 'subscribed an agreement to take banknotes in payment'. The Bank, Ryder wrote, 'acted imprudently in taking fright so soon', and yet even after being rescued by the merchants, continued, 'paying in silver, which occasioned a decay in credit'. Newcastle wrote to his friend the Duke of Richmond:

> I am very apprehensive, that the Pretender, being in possession of Scotland may encourage France to try to put them in possession of England also . . . Everything is done that can be done by an Administration that has no power, and to whom the King, their master, will hardly vouchsafe to say one word about his own business. The greater the danger is, the more angry he grows with those who alone can help him out of it, and if he goes on he may run the risk of losing another kingdom by the rashness and hating of some as he has already done one by the folly and obstinacy of others.

To the Whigs, who, of course, sincerely believed that the Hanoverian succession was the only guarantee for the constitution, the situation was appalling. Charles Yorke, Lord Chancellor Hardwicke's son, commented:

> It is indeed a dreadful and amazing consideration to reflect that the work of so many wise and honest men, and of so many Parliaments of fifty seven years, that a fabric of so much art and cost at the Revolution and its train of consequences, should be in danger of being overwhelmed by the bursting of a cloud, which seemed, at first gathering, no bigger than a man's hand.

The addresses from all parts of England did not give him much comfort, for, as he wrote, 'The Gazettes about the time of the Revolution are filled with very handsome ones to King James!'[1]

Upon the first news of His Royal Highness's arrival, Sempill wrote:

> The City of London, Sir John Hynde Cotton, Lord Barrymore, the Duke of Beaufort, and all the English cry loudly and vehemently for a body of troops to be landed near London, as the most effectual means to support the Prince, and the only method by which a dangerous and ruinous civil war can be avoided.

[1] Coxe, *Horatio, Lord Walpole* ii 111; Owen 228–83; *HMC 14th Rep.* ix 131, 132; Northumberland mss., A. Mordaunt to Lady Hertford, 19 Sept. 1745; Ryder diary 14 August, 20, 26, 28 September 1745, 5 January 1746; Add. 47098Bff. 6, 9, 10; Yorke, *Hardwicke* i 417, 458, 462; *HMC* i 115.

They were unable to act without 'a body of troops to support them' but 'would join the Prince if His Highness could force his way to them'. In the City of London 'Alderman Heathcote, and several more, have been with Sir Watkins, to assure him that they will rise in the city of London at the same time. He begs that arms and ammunition be brought with the troops.' Sir John Douglas, a Member of Parliament who was in London at the time, later told Charles Edward that Heathcote had collected £10,000 in the City against his arrival. Lefebure reported that there were then not 'above 10,000 regular troops' in England, but that eight battalions of foot from Flanders were expected at Newcastle, and that the 6,000 Hessians in English pay were bound to be sent for.[1]

Charles Edward had, in fact, never had any intention of doing without French assistance. As soon as he had landed, he wrote to Louis XV, informing him of his arrival and asking him to send arms and troops to Scotland. In order to counteract the use Whig propaganda would make of his appeal to France, he counterattacked vigorously in his proclamation issued from Edinburgh on 11 October:

> The fears of the nation from the powers of France and Spain appear still more vain and groundless. My expedition was undertaken unsupported by either: but, indeed, when I see a foreign force brought by my enemies against me, and when I hear of Dutch, Danes, Hessians and Swiss, the Elector of Hanover's allies, being called over to protect his government against the King's subjects, is it not high time for the King my father to accept also of the assistance of those who are able and who have engaged to support him? But will the world, or any one man of sense in it, infer from thence that he inclines to be a tributary prince rather than an independent monarch? Who has the better chance to be independent of foreign powers? He who, with the aid of his own subjects, can wrest the government out of the hands of an intruder or he who cannot, without assistance from abroad, support his government, though established by all the civil power, and secured by a strong military force, against the undisciplined part of those he has ruled over so many years? Let him, if he pleases, try the experiment; let him send of his foreign hirelings, and put the whole upon the issue of a battle. I will trust to the King my father's subjects, who are, or shall be, engaged in mine and their country's cause.

[1] Stuart mss. 268/5; 269/109; *HC* i 618; Browne iii 446–7, 450–1.

France, who had already sent arms, ammunition, money, officers and a few troops to Scotland, was preparing a larger scale force, and the Pretender's younger son, Henry Duke of York had already arrived in France to lead it. Boyer, Marquis d'Eguilles, the brother of the Marquis d'Argens later French ambassador at the Court of Berlin, arrived by 15 October at Edinburgh as accredited envoy to Charles Edward as regent of Scotland and the ally of France. Lord Elcho's statement that Boyer 'had not the least authority from the Court of France' is simply preposterous. On 13/24 October 1745 France had signed the Treaty of Fontainebleau with the Pretender, by which she ceased to recognise the Elector of Hanover as King of Great Britain; promised to send military assistance to Charles Edward; recognised James VIII as King of Scotland and undertook to recognise him as King of England as soon as this could be shown to be the wish of the nation and a free Parliament. Eguilles wrote to the Marquis d'Argenson, the French foreign minister, that the Prince now wanted troops sent to England, and asked France to find ways of putting pressure on the Dutch to withdraw their troops. As it turned out the Dutch troops sent to England had undertaken, under the terms of the capitulation of Tournai, not to serve against France or her allies, and were forced to withdraw, so that Charles Edward did not find them in Lancashire. He wrote to his father from Edinburgh on 15 October:

> I wish to God I may find my brother landed in England by the time I enter it, which will be about ten days, having with me near 8000 men, and 300 horse at least, with which, as matters stand, I should have one decisive stroke for it, but if the French land, perhaps none.

To the Duc de Richelieu, who was to lead the expedition into England, he wrote later that his main object in entering England was to make a junction with him and his brother in the south, preferably near London.[1]

On 9 October the attorney general and solicitor general had begun to prepare a bill to suspend the Habeas Corpus Act in readiness for the meeting of Parliament on the 17th. Wynn, Cotton,

[1] AEM & D. Ang. 77f. 47; Ewald i 238–9; Ld. Elcho, *An Account of the Affair of Scotland* (1973 ed.) 358; *Murray of Broughton* 436–7; AEM & D. Ang. 87ff. 191; 82ff. 128–9, 189–90; 78ff. 231, 316–7, 439–42; Mahon iii App. p. xxviii; Stuart mss. 269/191.

Barrymore and the rest attended, for if they had not they were liable to arrest on suspicion of treason as well as for being absent from the service of the House. It was reported that the Government had sent instructions to governors of towns, justices, and local officials to watch for signs of disaffection. In Yorkshire, Staffordshire and the northern counties, orders were sent to search the houses and papers of suspected persons and arrest them if needs be. In Flintshire, Newcastle wanted reports not only of those who might favour the Pretender but also of those who cursed King George! Even in London, Wynn and Barrymore were being tailed by Newcastle's spies. Sir John Philipps moved an unsuccessful amendment to the loyal address to pass first a bill 'for securing his Majesty's faithful subjects the perpetual enjoyment of their undoubted right to be freely and fairly represented in Parliament, frequently chosen, and exempted from undue influence of every kind', declaring 'the addresses of the people of England are already become a proverb among our foreign neighbours; and if we go on but a few years as we have done, the addresses of our Parliament will fall under the same reproach.' The suspension of the Habeas Corpus Act moved the same day met, Horace Walpole wrote, 'with obstructions from the Jacobites. By this we may expect what spirit they will show hereafter.' In the Lords Westmorland said the Act had never been suspended under William and Anne except just after the Revolution, but now it was being for ever suspended on 'the least pretence'.[1] All over England, Associations were being formed in defence of the King and the Government and subscriptions to raise additional forces collected. On limited evidence, since these have never been studied systematically, the response of Tories varied according to counties. Horatio Walpole wrote, that many Tories 'for fear of being suspected, joined in the Associations, and a great many in the subscriptions', as did most Roman Catholics. Humphrey Sydenham, a high Tory, complained in Parliament that pressure was being put on Tories to take both subscriptions and Associations under threat of being branded as traitors if they did not. In Oxfordshire, one of the strongest Tory counties in England, the Tories did not take them. In Shropshire, none of the Tory gentlemen appeared at the county meeting or

[1] Ryder diary 9, 18 Oct. 1745; SP 36/76/45 and 152–65; *CJ* xxv 4; *H. Walpole Corresp.* xix 106–7; *Parl. Hist.* xiii 1322, 1353.

took the Association. In Derbyshire, Tories, including Sir Nathaniel Curzon, took the subscriptions. In Yorkshire the Archbishop of York was very active in organising the Association and subscriptions, and it was reported 'the Yorkshire gentlemen have had the greatest meeting that ever was known to shew their zeal for the Government, and several Tories took them, though some of the aldermen of York were suspected as disaffected', rightly since two of them had offered to send the freedom of the city in a gold box to the Duke of York the year before. The Archbishop himself did not take these at their face value, writing to Hardwicke that 'we had very gallant professions of zeal and unanimity but *quid verba audiam cum facta non videam*'. In London, George Heathcote had tried to get the grand jury of Middlesex to present the Associations and subscriptions as illegal (a device used by the Whigs in 1680 to present the Duke of York as a Papist) and he failed by one vote, while in Parliament he and Thomas Carew compared them to the 'benevolences of Charles I's time'. Wynn also subscribed as a precaution. Charles Edward, on his side, declared himself—

traduced, misrepresented and reviled in those fulsome addresses and associations made to and in favour of the Elector of Hanover, by those very bishops of the Church of England, who, for so many years, have contributed their utmost endeavours to abet and support every measure the most unpopular, pernicious, and hurtful, and that the worst of ministers, be he of what party he would, could ever devise for the undoing of these nations.[1]

Lord Perceval wrote that Lord Gower had been to see the King 'and assured him that he had formerly been his enemy and a Jacobite, but he saw the folly of it and that he be no more', and offered to raise a regiment in Staffordshire for him. The Duke of Bedford and several other Whig noblemen followed suit. However, the gesture was somewhat spoilt when, according to Horace Walpole, it was noticed that these 'most disinterested colonels' had filled these

---

[1] *Parl. Hist.* xiii 1351–2; R. J. Robson, *The Oxfordshire Election of 1754* 2; Chatsworth mss., Lord Herbert to Duke of Devonshire, 10 Oct. 1745; Newcastle to Devonshire, 11 Oct. 1745; Northumberland mss., A. Mordaunt to Lady Hertford, 19 Sept. and 9 Oct. 1745; C. Collier, 'Yorkshire and the Forty Five', *Yorkshire Archaeological Journal* xxxviii 71–95; *Murray of Broughton* 41; P. Thomas, *Jacobitism in Wales* 297; Browne iii 113–14.

regiments with their relations and friends and expected them to have rank in the Army, and this was strongly opposed by 'the Jacobites and Patriots', the last by now were only Cobham's cubs. The commanders of these newly raised regiments were satirised by Sir Charles Hanbury Williams, a Whig, in *The Heroes: A new Ballad* published at this time, in which Gower was advised to reflect:

> And now, dear G . . ., thou man of Pow'r,
> And comprehensive Noodle;
> Tho' you've the Gout, yet as you're stout,
> Why wa'n't you plac'd in Saddle?
> Then you might ride to either Side,
> Chuse which K . . . you'd serve under;
> But, dear Dragoon, charge not too soon,
> For fear of th'other Blunder.[1]

One of the most remarkable features of the '45 is that while Charles Edward was in touch with the French and with his father throughout, he never once managed to establish contact with the Tory leaders. He had not consulted them before landing in Scotland, had established no safe channel of communication, didn't even know where they were. On 22 September, the day after the battle of Prestonpans in late September, he sent a messenger into Northumberland with the following message:

You are thereby authorised to repair forthwith into England, and there to notify my friends, and particularly those in the north and north-west, the wonderful success with which it had hitherto pleased God to favour my endeavours for their deliverance. You are to let them know that it is my full intention, in a few days, to move towards them; and that they will be inexcusable before God and man if they do not do all in their power to assist and support me in such an undertaking. What I demand and expect is, that as many of them as can, shall be ready to join me, and that they should take care to furnish provisions and money, that the country may suffer as little as possible by the march of my troops. Let them know that there is no time for deliberation—now or never is the word. I am resolved to conquer or perish. If this last should happen, let them judge what they and their posterity have to expect.

[1] Add. 47098Bf. 11. *H. Walpole Corresp.* xix 153; Chatsworth mss., Lord Hartington to Devonshire, 5 Nov. 1745.

It never got through as the messenger was arrested. The rebel army crossed into England on 8 November, and three days later he sent the following letter to Lord Barrymore at Marbury in Cheshire, sending it by two messengers:

> This is to acquaint you with the success we have had since our arrival in Scotland, and how far we are advanced without repulse. We are now a numerous army, and are laying siege to Carlisle this day . . . After that we intend to take our route straight to London, and if things answer our expectations we design to be in Cheshire before the 24th inst. Then I hope you and all my friends in the county will be ready to join us. For now is the time or never.

They got to Marbury only to be told that Barrymore was in London, but that his eldest son Lord Buttevant was there to whom they gave the letter. Now Barrymore's relationship with his eldest son was Hanoverian and Buttevant sided with the Government, handing over letter and messengers. Barrymore later repaid him by letting him rot in prison for debt! The Prince wrote a letter which was also intercepted, apparently meant for Wynn at Wynnstay:

> After the success which providence has granted to my arms in Scotland, I thought I could not do better than to enter England, where I have always been assured that I should meet with many friends, equally disposed to exert their loyalty to their native king, and to shake off a foreign yoke under which the nation has so long groaned. I have now put into their hands an opportunity to doing both, by repairing with what strength every man can to my army, from which the enemy industriously keeps at such a distance. The particular character I have heard of you, makes me hope to see you among the first. I am persuaded you will not baulk my expectations, and you need not doubt but I shall always remember to your advan' tage the example you shall thus have put to your neighbours, and consequently to all England.[1]

Whereas every aspect of the rebellion in Scotland has been covered, and every Jacobite prisoner identified, English response

---

[1] Chatsworth mss.; Ewald i 260, 274–5, 277; *HC* i 441–2; *HMC Egmont diary* iii 317.

to the rebellion has hardly been touched upon. Obviously the amount of sympathy there was in England cannot be known, how can one quantify views which cannot be expressed? To make matters worse, as the situation became tenser, most Whig sources dry up. Newspapers printed only Whig propaganda. Letters from the North and Midlands were held up by the Government, and in the absence of solid news, it was believed in London that 'all Manchester to a man had joined the rebels'. The agent of the Duke of Devonshire in Derbyshire thought that the disaffected would rise only if 'any foreign force should land'. It is true that a small number of Englishmen joined the rebels, but more did join than Elcho and the two Murrays assert. Only two are said to have done so in Northumberland, neither of any consequence; yet a list of the tenants of the Duke of Somerset who joined the rebels, sent by his steward at Alnwick, alone contains over a dozen names, including those of Thomas Forster of Etherstone (son of the Jacobite general of the '15), Edward Blackett, John Clavering, and Sir Nicholas Sherburn, a Roman Catholic, the historic names of Northumberland. An English gentleman called Clifton, who came to France in early January 1746 with a pass from the English Government as his wife was dying there, and whose account of the situation in Cheshire and Derbyshire tallies with that from government sources, said that there were at Derby 1,500 Englishmen with the Prince, and he could have had large numbers in Lancashire especially had he been able to provide them with arms and officers. This agrees with what Lochiel (who was there) later said to Charles Edward:

> Your Royal Highness is not ignorant, that, both before and during the time of your last attempt, your English friends were ready and willing to declare for you, if you could either have furnished them with arms, or brought a body of troops capable to protect them.[1]

The general attitude of Englishmen before Derby, was very much one of wait and see until it was clear who would come out

---

[1] C. S. Terry, *The Forty Five* 78; Northumberland mss. 'a particular account of his Grace's tenants . . . in the rebellion'; A. Mordaunt to Lady Hertford, 3 Dec. 1745; Chatsworth mss., John Griffith to Devonshire, 25 Sept. 1745; Guerre A1/1352/167 and 177; Browne iii 489.

on top, and this is easy to understand in view of the penalty of being caught on the wrong side of a civil war. The Whigs who had been given arms by the Government were not keen to use them. Cumberland was a Whig county, but when the Whig governor wanted to defend Carlisle, the militia absolutely insisted on surrendering, and some of the local aldermen were accused of having carried the keys of the city to offer them to Charles Edward at Brampton. In Lancashire, where the Whigs had made a good showing in the '15, Lord Derby the lord lieutenant disbanded the militia as he could find neither officers nor recruits. The same applied to Cheshire where Lord Cholmondeley reported to Newcastle that as the rebels approached 'I found despair, fear and confusion had seized the minds of everyone so that when the danger came nearer, not a justice was to be found, or gentlemen of estate to do any one act for the safety or protection of it'. The most notorious example was the Derbyshire Blues, the regiment raised by the Duke of Devonshire, who when ordered by the duke to march against the rebels 'to a man refused him'. Similarly when Sir Richard Wrottesley raised a troop of yeomanry and set out to join his father-in-law Lord Gower's regiment, his men would go no farther than the nearest inn, less than a mile from their starting point.[1]

At Preston, which the rebels entered on 26 November, Charles Edward was greeted 'by a great concourse of people and welcomed with the loudest shouts and acclamations of joy'. At Manchester, which local sympathisers contrived to hand over on the 30th, there were illuminations and ringing of bells, and they were joined 'by some young men of the most reputable families in the town, several substantial tradesmen and farmers, and above a hundred common men', 300 altogether who presumably had or were given arms, and were led by Francis Townley a Roman Catholic of an old Lancashire family who had military experience, having served in an Irish regiment in France. No doubt Charles Edward's popularity was enhanced by the fact that he had attended Protestant services ever since landing, and that Lord Elcho told the Lancashire people that the Prince's religion 'was to seek'. Sir Thomas Abney, a Whig judge, wrote to the Duke of Devonshire at this time 'the joy that I

[1] Mounsey 52–96, 204–5; Northumberland mss., A. Mordaunt to Lady Hertford, 10 Dec. 1745; SP 36/40/118; *HC* ii 143–4, 439, 559.

observed on the countenances of too many persons in the several counties I went through on the Oxford circuit gives me great uneasiness'. According to Clifton, the Government was very angry at the welcome the rebels were given in Lancashire, Staffordshire and Nottinghamshire. People's conduct was far from uniform: the treasurer of the Derbyshire subscriptions, Samuel Heathcote, who was Sir Nathaniel Curzon's steward, ended up being taken prisoner to London on a charge of high treason. He had not only tried to prevent the escape of a spy on the rebels sent by the Duke of Cumberland, but had ordered him to be shot through the head if found.[1]

London's reaction to the rebellion has long interested historians, but, as one of them noted, since it never got to London the real feelings of Londoners were never put to the test.[2] Recent work purporting to show that Jacobites in London consisted mainly of Irish Roman Catholics would seem to illustrate rather the usual behaviour of Irishmen in public houses.[3] Pitt later reflected that if the rebels 'had obtained a victory and made themselves masters of London, I question if the spirit of the population would not have taken a different turn'.[4] Some of the most interesting descriptions of London in the first week of December are in French sources; from a London merchant who came to France; from a Captain Nagle, an Irish officer in Lally's regiment, as well as information derived from the smugglers. They all describe London at this time as a ghost town, with the shops and playhouses shut, and noblemen dismissing half their servants. Nagle made his way to see a Lord whose name he left blank (perhaps Orrery, who was in touch with Lally) who told him they were all being watched and lying low in full expectation that Charles Edward would make his way to them or that the French and the Duke of York would land, and they would then take off the mask and that people never suspected

---

[1] James Maxwell of Kirkconnel 70; David Daiches, *Charles Edward Stuart* 106–7; Howell, *State Trials* xviii 371; Eardley Simpson 97; Guerre A1/3152/157; Chatsworth mss., affidavit by E. Birch of 23 Dec. 1745; SP 36/76/93; SP 36/76/339–40.

[2] George Rudé, *Hanoverian London* 155.

[3] N. Rogers, 'Popular disaffection in London during the Forty Five', *London Journal* i 1–26.

[4] Sharpe, *London and the Kingdom* iii 50–6. See also A. A. Mitchell, 'London and the Forty Five', *History Today* Nov. 1965, 719–26.

before would declare for the Prince. Meanwhile, both sides drank
the healths of 'the King, the Prince, the Duke' without naming
names. Lord Cobham was reported to have said in public of
Charles Edward that the young man has not put a foot wrong since
he landed, and would be a great man if he were not a Papist.
Wynn had been questioned by the Government, but had escaped
arrest as the Duke of Bedford had vouched for him.[1] Official
sources in England show that a government spy reported that
Lefebure had been seeing Jacobites, but this was not followed up
by Newcastle. The Pretender's declaration of 23 December 1743
and Charles Edward's proclamations were being printed and
distributed in London, and though they were ceremoniously burnt
by the hangman at the Royal Exchange, Newcastle was never able
to catch more than one of the persons responsible for them.[2]
To everyone's surprise the Duke of Norfolk was seen at Court 'to
clear himself of his steward being gone over to the rebels' and his
visit, though not the reason for it, was put in the *Gazette* 'that the
disaffected and Roman Catholics may see it'. Sir Robert Grosvenor,
a friend of Wynn and member of the Jacobite Cycle of the White
Rose, also went, 'having never been there before and always counted
very high', either to reinsure his immense wealth or for a reason
similar to the Duke of Norfolk's. Beaufort's man of affairs David
Morgan (see below) had already joined Charles Edward, perhaps
an illustration of Walpole's prophecy 'if you see them come again,
they will begin by their lowest people; their chiefs will not appear
till the end'.[3]

The position of Charles Edward and his army at Derby in the
first week of December and the decision of whether to march on
London must be seen not only in the light of the reaction of people
in the North and the Midlands but against the position and strength
of the Government forces, the psychological factors operating at
the time, and whether there was any serious prospect of assistance
from France.

General Wade, who had been at Newcastle was now at Doncaster, several days march away and showed no sign of moving.

[1] Guerre AI/3152/167, 170, 171, 174, 189, 196.
[2] SP 36/78/12, 18 and 154.
[3] Northumberland mss., A. Mordaunt to Lady Hertford, 10 Dec. 1745; SP
36/76/274; *H. Walpole Corresp.* xix 118.

A veteran of Steinkirk in 1692, Wade was now in his seventies. Newcastle said that Wade 'was timid, and had always black atoms before his eyes'. A military historian has rightly said that Wade's favourite tactic was 'masterly inertia'. Henry Pelham commented earlier on:

> I dare say the old man will act for the best, and if he can come to a fair field of battle, I should not despair of success. We must hope for the best. I pray God this may be soon decided, for if it is not, all our accounts from abroad open a sad scene. It is pretty certain that France will support the Pretender openly, and I hear from good hands that the Duke of Richelieu and most of their favourite officers are destined for this service. Amidst these general misfortunes, I cannot help mentioning our particular situations at home. The King frightened yet impracticable and some of our new Allies [in Parliament] filled with the most extraordinary notions, and even now stipulating before hand, what we shall or shall not do with regard to foreign affairs, before the rebellion is put an end to.

Finding it impossible to get recruits for the army, the Cabinet asked the law officers to prepare a Pressing Act on the model of that of 1640. A second army of about 6,000 men under the Duke of Cumberland and the Duke of Richmond was sent to try and prevent the rebels getting to London. The newly raised regiments, in addition to these, were regarded as useless, Cumberland writing of Bedford's which was regarded as the best, 'neither men nor officers know what they are about, so how they will do before an enemy God only knows'. Cumberland was confident he could get between the rebels and London. The Duke of Richmond did not share his optimism. In letters to Newcastle marked 'most secret' to be shown 'to nobody but the Chancellor and Mr. Pelham', Richmond complained that Wade was 'quite out of the way'; that the rebels were always too fast; that his army was 'marched to death' and could get no rest not daring to go into cantonment for fear of being attacked at night. At the very time of the retreat from Derby Richmond reported that he feared the rebels would get to London first:

> what in the name of wonder is become of Marshal Wade? . . . the rebels will certainly be two days march ahead of us . . . I make no doubt but this embarkation will go on at Dunkirk. Are we all mad?

that you don't send for ten thousand more forces be they Hessians, Hanoverians, or devils, if they will but fight for us . . . The whole kingdom is still asleep. Our cavalry can't be here before February, and the Pretender may be crowned at Westminster by that time.[1]

The psychological advantage of Charles Edward and his army at this stage was enormous. Horace Walpole, who had treated the rebellion lightly at first began to say, 'sure banditti can never conquer a kingdom. On the other hand, what can't any number of men do that meet with no opposition; they have hitherto taken no place but open towns.' A Whig clergyman who escaped from Carlisle reflected that it seemed as if Heaven 'had made all opposition either to fall before them, or to become ineffectual'. In London, the news that Charles Edward was at Derby came on Black Friday, 6 December, when Philip Yorke wrote to his brother who was with Cumberland's army:

The motion of the rebels to Derby threw us into no small panic here lest they should give you the slip as they had done Mr. Wade and get to London by hasty marches. Our alarm was much increased by the news of a large embarkation at Dunkirk, which was intended for the south and in concert with the Young Pretender to land near the capital. The same terror but in a higher degree (as the strength to resist was less) has spread itself through all parts of the kingdom and to every great town, on every road which it was possible for the rebels to take in on their way to London.[2]

Ever since his first landing in Scotland, Charles Edward had been appealing for French help, but having neither consulted nor concerted anything with them it was not until the middle of October that any serious plans to give it were made and not until mid-November that preparations began in earnest. They were then still planning to send troops to Scotland and the *Royal Ecossais* under Lord John Drummond had already left for Montrose via Ostend when Sir James Stewart arrived in France from the Prince

<hr />

[1] Chatsworth mss., H. Pelham to Devonshire, 19 Nov. 1745; George Wade to Devonshire, Doncaster 8 Dec. 1745; W. T. Waugh, *James Wolfe* 46; Ryder diary 21 Dec. 1745; Add. 32705ff. 360–1, 362, 365, 409, 411, 421–3.

[2] *H. Walpole Corresp.* xix 109–110; Mounsey 125; Add. 35363f. 109; Yorke, *Hardwicke* i 477.

to ask that no more troops be sent to Scotland and all available troops be sent to England, whereupon the Fitzjames regiment ready to embark at Ostend was recalled.[1]

In London Cotton and Barrymore sent a message through Dr Barry and Lefebure asking the French to land troops in Essex as first arranged in 1744 'on account of its vicinity to London and the facility of joining them', adding:

> The King's friends entreat in the most earnest and pressing manner that the troops be sent without delay there being nothing at present to obstruct the expedition for Admiral Vernon has only two frigates with him. Lord Barrymore desires he may have some warning in order to secure himself and the King's friends.

They asked that spare arms be brought over, and undertook to meet the Duke of York and the troops on landing. At this stage they were asked through Lord Clancarty to give assurances under their own hands, but this once more they refused to do for reasons explained to the Pretender:

> The sentiments and inclinations of Sir Watkin, Lord Barrymore, and their friends, are known to all, they intend they should and even use means to manifest them; but they, with great reason, make a vast distinction between the owning of their principles, and being engaged in any direct or indirect correspondence with Your Majesty and the French Court, with an actual design of overturning the present government; the owning of their principles exposes them only to the hatred of an administration from which they neither expect nor desire any favour, but a correspondence of the nature I have mentioned, is an overt act of treason according to the present laws, the least suspicion of which would bring certain ruin upon them, and consequently render them insignificant and useless to Your Majesty's cause, whereas they have all along kept it awake, and can by their influence and example to determine above two-thirds of the nation to act vigorously for it, as soon as they see a probability, nay, even a possibility of success.

All letters to the Pretender and to Sempill from England were signed in cypher only. Instead, Sir John Cotton offered to resign his place as a pledge of earnestness. He was not asked to do so then,

[1] Marine B3/429/256, 267, 268, 353, 356, 368, 384, 406; Marine B3/426/661; Guerre A1/3152/16, 22, 23, 24.

but according to Chesterfield Cotton's resignation was to be the
sign from England for the embarkation to begin. How Chesterfield
learned this can only be surmised. He was then lord lieutenant of
Ireland, writing to Newcastle before Derby that the rebellion
caused him not the least alarm, and that there was no need to send
for more troops from abroad. Ryder noted in his diary that Chesterfield had refused an offer from the Irish House of Commons to
raise 6,000 troops to be sent to England.[1]

The refusal to give signatures proved no obstacle since the new
Secretary of State for Foreign Affairs René Louis de Voyer, Marquis
d'Argenson, had been a warm partisan of a restoration of the
Stuarts since 1739. He was the elder brother of the Comte d'Argenson the minister for war, but very different in character. An idealist,
who frequented clubs used by the *Philosophes*, he was interested
in projects for universal peace and his own philosophical writings
were later used by Jean Jacques Rousseau. His schoolfriend
Voltaire nicknamed him secretary of state for Plato's republic.
In charge of the expedition to England at his own request was
Louis François Armand du Plessis, Duc de Richelieu, great grand-
nephew of Cardinal Richelieu, and the intimate friend of Louis XV.
The Don Juan of eighteenth-century France and the patron of
Voltaire, Richelieu was a freethinker who, as governor of Languedoc
had stopped the persecution of the Protestants, and was in 1756 to
capture Minorca from Admiral Byng. When the English ministers
learned of the appointment Ryder noted that Richelieu, a prime
favourite at the French court was not going to be sent to *Scotland*.[2]
Having taken the decision, Louis XV and his ministers, as a witness
at the court of Versailles wrote, worked on nothing and thought of
nothing but the expedition to England. It was planned on a bigger
scale than the 1744 attempt, with about 12,000 troops altogether,
and this time consisted of Irish regiments including those commanded by General Bulkeley, a relation of James 6th Viscount
Bulkeley [I] Wynn's friend in Wales; by Viscount Dillon;

[1] Stuart mss. 270/51, 105, 142; 271/3; AEM & D. Ang. 77ff. 246–7, 335–6;
Walpole, *Memoirs of George II* ii 103; Add. 32804ff. 379–83; Ryder diary 1 Jan.
and 6 Mar. 1746.

[2] Argenson ii 264 and passim; Balteau; *Mémoires authentiques du duc de
Richelieu*, ed. Boislisle. For Richelieu's administration of Languedoc, see Bibliothèque de Rouen, Collection Leber ms. 3344; Ryder diary Oct. 1745.

Lichfield's brother-in-law, Lord Clare; and included the Duke and Count of Fitzjames, James II's grandsons; as well as the Prince de Turenne and other French noblemen. The military arrangements were placed under Lally, colonel of an Irish regiment, working with Anthony Walshe and Lord Clancarty (now vice-admiral in the French navy) who were organising all naval preparations. Unlike Charles Edward in 1744, Henry Duke of York, who was to be in nominal charge of the landing, was received at Versailles with great ceremony, but Richelieu was not impressed by him, objecting particularly to his 'Italianate devotion' which was having an adverse effect on the Protestant officers in the expedition. The death of Ormonde, who had been once again asked to take part, in late November was particularly regretted by Barrymore 'inasmuch as the Duke's age and rank set him above all jealousies and envy, an advantage no other subject can pretend to'.[1]

The French were well aware that their plans in 1744 had been betrayed to the English Government and, unaware that their own man Bussy was responsible, thought the Tories in England had been indiscreet. So that, while outwardly agreeing with Sir John Cotton's proposal of a descent at Maldon in Essex, they decided that the real places of landing were to be Folkestone, Hythe and Romney, and that Cotton and his friends should not be told until the very last minute. Similarly, to deceive the English Government, elaborate shows of preparation were made at Dunkirk and Ostend, but the real places of embarkation were to be Calais and Boulogne. Since Bussy never gave any more information after the declaration of war with England, the feint worked, and all along the Pelhams believed that the embarkation was preparing at Dunkirk. Walshe used only ships under 30 tons capable of landing in shallow waters to transport the troops, drawing these from Calais, Ambleuteuse, Boulogne, St. Valéry-en-Somme, Dieppe and Fécamp. An escort of warships he thought would be more of a danger than a protection as it would alert the English fleet, and since they could rely on the smugglers to tell them when the coast was clear and to act as pilots. The Marquis d'Argenson worked out that the operation immobilised most of French commercial shipping in the northern ports and cost France about five million

[1] Guerre AI/3152/46, 48, 52, 186 and 225; Marine B3/429/384, 385, 416 and 417; Luynes vii 142-3, 152-3, 156-7; Stuart mss. 271/51; Argenson iv 319-20.

livres. The Council of State thought that since England and France were now at war, there was no need to draw up a manifesto to distribute on landing, but Richelieu disagreed, writing:

> If our object was to subjugate the English and to conquer England, there would be no need for a manifesto since we are at war, but as we are counting less on the force of our arms and the number of our troops than on the party which will support us among the nation, it seems to be of the highest importance to explain clearly to the English in which spirit we are come, and that we arrive less to fight than to succour them.

Thereupon, he and the Marquis d'Argenson commissioned Voltaire to write it and had it printed in English and French. This declared that the Duc de Richelieu was landing at the head of French troops at the request of persons of great consideration in England; that they would be withdrawn as soon as the legitimate king was restored; and that Prince Charles Edward's only object was to maintain the laws and liberties and to secure the happiness of his subjects. Bussy, who was consulted when the declaration was drawn, made every possible objection to the policy of restoring the Stuarts, presumably because he knew he faced certain discovery if it succeeded. The Marquis d'Argenson, who had formed a warm friendship for Charles Edward, whom he regarded as 'a hero and a man of sense', used Voltaire's pen at this time to mount a full-scale public relations campaign on his behalf in Europe. The Duke of York sent his brother the following letter which reached him at Manchester:

> The Marquis d'Argenson in a conference with me a few days ago told me I might send immediately to advise you in his name and his brother's [the Comte d'Argenson] that the King of France was absolutely resolved upon the expedition into England *qu'il y avoit mis le bon*, and that you might count upon it being ready the 20th of December new style [9 December o.s.].[1]

---

[1] AI/3152/62; AEM & D. Ang. 77f. 224; 78ff. 213, 224-5, 381, 389; Marine B3/426/677 and 687; 82ff. 166-70, 173-9; Voltaire, *Oeuvres Complètes*, ed. Beuchot, xxxviii 543; L. Bongie, 'Voltaire's English, high treason and a manifesto for Bonnie Prince Charles', *Studies on Voltaire and the eighteenth century* clxxi (1977) 7-29; Argenson iv 316-20; Ewald i 278-9.

On his own initiative, the Duke of York wrote to Sir Watkin Williams Wynn in London, suggesting that he and his friends should assist the French landing by seizing a seaport. When James heard of this some time later, he wrote to the Duke:

> I suppose you took all proper precautions that your letter to Sir Watkins Williams might come safely to his hands; but I don't see how it is possible for our friends in England to order what you propose to them, for how can they, without arms, without regular troops, without enfin, any support, pretend to rise in arms, and much less to seize on any seaport, while the government have so many regular troops in this island, and at present, even a considerable body near London. I have often blamed the indolence and timidity of our friends in England; but, in the present moment, I own I think they would act imprudently and even rashly not to lie quiet still.

Richelieu, who had not been consulted, could not see how unarmed civilians could be expected to capture a seaport, and if they could, it would be no help to him as it would pinpoint the place of landing. He was much more sympathetic to the difficulties of James's friends in England than the Comte de Saxe had been, telling Bulkeley who was blaming their 'timidity' that people could not be bold when surrounded by regular troops. All he asked of them, he said, was that they should join him when he landed. There were delays, partly because the locks of the canals on which equipment was being taken to Calais and Boulogne froze, and partly because French army and navy officials insisted on their six months' supply of everything, despite Walshe's objection that this was far too much. The date on which the expedition was to sail was the night of 14/25 December 1745.[1]

Thus the rebels could count on massive reinforcements if they marched South—provided these reinforcements could get across the Channel. The admiral to whom the task of preventing the French landing had been entrusted was Admiral Edward Vernon, an able commander, and one of the few admirals of his time who showed any real concern for the welfare of his men. His effectiveness, however, was diminished by the fact that he was

[1] Marine B3/429/456, 457, 458 and 470; Guerre A1/3152/167, 174, 177, 195, 204, 205; Browne iii 456–7; Argenson iv 318 (writing many years later his chronology is inexact); Stuart mss. 271/150.

continually at odds with the Lords of the Admiralty, and that both were at this time repeatedly at cross-purposes. It was one of the many ironies of the situation that he was confiding his difficulties with the Admiralty to Sir John Philipps, a Jacobite closely associated with Wynn and those inviting the French invasion. With only a limited force at his disposal, some of his ships too large for narrow seas, and the ten Dutch ships seconded to him withdrawn by Holland under pressure from France, he was asked by the Admiralty to blockade Dunkirk and Ostend, as well as to protect the Downs and the coasts of Kent, Sussex, and East Anglia. He considered a close blockade of enemy ports impracticable: 'For my part, I have always looked upon pretending to block up the port of Dunkirk from their privateers getting out in the winter time to be a little better than the labour of the wise men of Gotham for hedging in the cuckoo.' It would have been no use if he had, since Dunkirk was not the real port of embarkation. Moreover, Vernon believed the French designed to land in Suffolk, and concentrated his resources on a squadron to cover the mouth of the Thames and the coasts of Norfolk and Suffolk, but there again the French did not intend to land there. Quite rightly, he complained that the French had the advantage of good intelligence 'from their friends and spies the smugglers' and that 'there is not the least thing done or ordered but the enemy immediately knows it by their means'. As things were, therefore, the French expedition had a good chance of getting through.[1]

On 5 December the leaders of the rebel army called a council of war at Derby to decide whether to march on London with about 6,000 men. David Morgan, a barrister who acted as legal adviser to the 3rd and 4th Dukes of Beaufort, and was a leading member of the Association of Independent Electors of Westminster, had joined them at Preston. He advised them:

> It would be an easy matter to march forward for London, for there were not above 3000 soldiers between them and London and most of them dragoons besides a few undisciplined troops that were raised by Lord Gower and Lord Cholmondeley who would make but little opposition.

[1] *H. Walpole Corresp.* xix 168; *HMC 14th Rep.* ix 138–9; *Vernon Papers* (Navy Records Society) 439, 540–4, 550, 555, 560, 568, 571 and 575.

Apart from the Guards who were few in number, the defenders of London had a comic opera quality, illustrated in Hogarth's *The March to Finchley*, and Pelham himself did not think London could be defended. Charles Edward told Lord George Murray and the others that his objective all along had been London; that they could get there before Cumberland; that he was sure he would be made as welcome there as he had been in Edinburgh; and that he had letters to show that the French under the Duke of York were about to land so that they would be reinforced. Boyer, the French envoy, told them 'he was confident the French would land and offered to be shot if they did not land in a fortnight's time'. Nothing succeeds like success, and at this point when everything was going their way and for reasons never made entirely clear, Charles Edward met with a blank wall of obstinacy from most of the leaders of his army, who forced him to retreat. Apart from the Duke of Perth and Sir William Gordon, the rest of the council absolutely refused to believe that a French expedition was about to come to their help, and objected, more reasonably, that few Englishmen of note had joined them. The real reason for their decision to retreat, however, was a narrow kind of Scottish nationalism. All along they had complained that Charles Edward was 'occupied with England' to the exclusion of Scotland the land of his ancestors, and some of them even told him 'they had taken arms and risked their fortunes and their hopes, merely to seat him on the throne of Scotland; but that they wished to have nothing to do with England.' The Chevalier Johnstone, a-d-c to Lord George Murray, even thought it would have been a good thing for the Prince to have fomented a 'national war' between England and Scotland! In his declaration, Charles Edward had promised to dissolve the Union, but he had no desire to be King of Scotland only, nor could he have been for how could an independent Scotland have been defended from King George and his allies? By forcing the retreat, Lord George Murray and the others threw away the best chance there had been of a restoration of the Stuarts, threw away all that the bravery of the Highlanders and their own military skill had achieved. The '45 was a gamble from the beginning, but they threw in their hand when they held most of the trump cards. Nor was this decision made under pressure from the clans, who had been reluctant to cross into England at first but were now in good spirits. They showed great indignation at being made to turn back; 'if we had been beaten,' wrote one of the rebels, 'the grief could not have been greater.' After quarrelling with Lord George Murray, Charles Edward declared:

> After this, I know that I have an army that I cannot command any farther than the chief officers please, and, therefore, if you are all resolved upon it, I must yield; but I take God to witness that it is with the greatest reluctance, and that I wash my hands of the fatal consequences which I foresee, but cannot help.

The retreat began the next day, and by 20 December they were back in Scotland. A good many of the English went home, a few like Morgan being denounced and caught as having been with the rebels. A substantial number garrisoned Carlisle and were taken when the Duke of Cumberland took it with Dutch troops (who had remained in England and began to act as soon as the rebels retreated), and other Englishmen marched to Scotland, to Culloden and inevitable doom. This time there were no deals in Scotland but terrible retribution and barbarous repression of the innocent as well as the guilty, and the heretable jurisdictions were abolished. Lord George Murray and Lord Elcho, assisted by Murray of Broughton, sought to evade responsibility for the consequences of the retreat. They blamed Charles Edward, the English, the French, everyone in fact except the lords of the council at Derby, and their statements have been accepted by historians all too uncritically.[1] Two days after the retreat, a messenger arrived in Derby from Barrymore and Wynn to say they would join in the capital or each in their own counties. Presumably the disarray in London was so great they felt free to act at last.[2]

The retreat from Derby came as an incredible relief to the English Government, who resumed the initiative at once. On 19 December the King sent a message to Parliament that:

---

[1] H. M. Vaughan 'Welsh Jacobitism', *Cymmrodorion Society* 1920–1, 29; Howell, *State Trials* xviii 371–91; SP 36/77/71; Lord Elcho, 302–5, 339–40; *Murray of Broughton* p. xxiii, 248, 432, 434; Yorke, *Hardwicke* i 477–8; Chevalier de Johnstone *Memoir of the Forty-five* (1820 ed.) 34–41, 45, 73; James Maxwell 73; Mounsey 152–3; SP 36/78/262; SP 36/80/160.

[2] *HC* i 442–3.

His Majesty having received undoubted intelligence, that preparations are making at Dunkirk, and other parts of France, which are
now in great forwardness, for invading this kingdom with a considerable number of forces, in support of the rebellion carrying on
here, in favour of the Pretender to his Crown; and some French
troops are actually landed in Scotland . . . His Majesty having the last
summer taken into his service 6000 Hessian troops . . . has judged it
necessary to direct the said Hessians to be brought into these
kingdoms.

Wynn and Heathcote took the unprecedented step of dividing
the House against the loyal address. In the debate, Gower and
his few followers spoke for the Hessians. Sir John Cotton and
his son were absent, 'kept away' by Gower according to one
source. Lord Cornbury declared his loyalty to the Crown but
objected to the use of foreign troops against his countrymen.
The Hessians came over within ten days, as well as additional
forces from Flanders all sent north after the rebels, and Wade was
replaced by 'Hangman Hawley'.[1]

The retreat to Scotland was the last thing the French had been
led to expect. On 14/25 December Richelieu, who was ready to
go, had not received the appointed signal from England and had
lost touch with Charles Edward. Officers from Lally's regiment
were sent over via the smugglers, reporting a great build up of
forces round London and the South East. Richelieu then consulted Bulkeley on the possibility of a landing in Wales, but the
reply was 'circumstances are sadly changed since the Prince of
Wales had marched back to Scotland'. On 18/29 December, two
of Vernon's privateers attacked and damaged two of the French
munition ships outside Calais. Richelieu looked on this as a
'minor setback', but Vernon had captured one of them and by
questioning the prisoners prised out of them the fact that the
embarkation was to go from Boulogne and Calais and from then
on English ships patrolled outside these two ports. At the end
of the month the enormous build-up of forces against his brother
led the Duke of York to ask the French to abandon the idea of an
expedition to England and to send all available help to Scotland.
Richelieu was even prepared to go there himself. James's friends

[1] *CJ* xxv 23; *Parl. Hist.* xiii 1392–3; Ld. Ilchester, *Life of Lord Holland* i 121.
HC ii 164–5.

in England made the same request early in January. At this time, Vernon who had for some time been asking to be relieved of his command was 'taken at his word', and an admiral working in harmony with the Admiralty succeeded in preventing the departure of any sizeable force. Whereas they could have hoped to slip across the Channel, an expedition to Scotland needed an escort of warships to defend it, and the Brest fleet was not ready to set out till April, so that they were reduced to send help to Scotland in single ships, some of which were taken and some of which arrived too late.[1]

[1] Guerre A1/3152/100, 103, 106, 146, 150, 152, 195 and 206; Marine B3/429/471 and 472; AEM & D. Ang. 78ff. 225, 402–3, 415; 85f. 159; *Vernon Papers* 578; Ryder diary 30 Dec. 1745 and 6 March 1746.

7

The Tory Backlash

Murray of Broughton, who had acted as Charles Edward's secretary during the rebellion, was captured after Culloden, and unlike the other Jacobite prisoners turned King's evidence to save his own life. Not only did he give evidence against the Scots with him in the rebellion, but he told the Government what he did not know of his own knowledge but only at second hand through Lord Traquair (whom he got excepted out of the Act of Indemnity) of the talks with Butler in 1743, naming Barrymore, Cotton, Wynn, Lord Orrery and Dr Barry and mentioning 'many persons in the City well affected to the Pretender' not identified by him, adding that they had continued to deal with the French in the relation to the Pretender's affairs in the years 1744–5. Either because Traquair did not tell him or for other reasons, Murray never mentioned Beaufort. The Cabinet at a meeting in February 1747 considered 'whether it might not be proper to communicate to the world by the help of the secret committee the information they had' concerning those named by Murray, but decided, as Lord Chancellor Hardwicke wrote, that 'satisfied with having brought the leaders of the rebellion to the block, and having the rest at their mercy, did not choose to push inquiries further'. In any case, not having two witnesses against them they could not have proceeded at law but only in Parliament by way of bill of attainder. True to form, the only person they arrested was Dr Barry, the underling. However, at the trial of Lord Lovat, one of the lords of the Association who had sent his clan out under his eldest son the Master of Fraser fairly late on in the rebellion and who was arrested and executed on Murray's evidence, the Government allowed the names of Barrymore, Wynn and Cotton to come out when the last two were present in the House. Thomas Prowse, a Tory Member who was not a Jacobite, objected that they should be allowed to speak in their own defence, but the Speaker replied 'that he believed the parties concerned would not choose it'. Nor did they![1]

Most of the Tory peers refused to attend the trials of the rebel lords. When, a Whig reported, Lord Chancellor Hardwicke told the 3rd Earl of Oxford he must attend,

> the other said he would not. The Chancellor with some warmth answered that the Lords would force him and being (asked) how, said by fine as they had done in the year 1715 and would be very severe. The other replied he would stand it all and go out of town, and I imagine all the other Tories will do the like.

Lord Foley, Horace Walpole said, 'withdrew as too well a wisher'. Most of the Tory peers writing to Hardwicke to be excused gave reasons of health, the only ones allowed and with a physician's certificate, but it is noticeable that whereas the Whig lords who would not attend prefaced their request with 'my loyalty to the Crown is too well known' or some such expression, not one of the Tory lords did so.[2] Beaufort, who had his windows broken for not illuminating his house in celebration of Culloden, apparently intended to attend Lovat's trial, in which Lovat named his brother the 3rd Duke as one of the people concerned on the English side. Lord Balmerino, one of the Scots, asked to be represented by Randle Wilbraham, a former protégé of Lord Gower, and 'a very able lawyer in the House of Commons, who, the Chancellor said privately, he was sure would be as soon hanged as plead such a cause', but he did. Richard Clayton, a lawyer returned as Member for Wigan by Lord Barrymore in 1747, acted as counsel for David Morgan who had been caught on an informer's evidence after the retreat from Derby. A complaint was made that John Williams, master of an inn where the witnesses against Lord Lovat were kept, had been abused and 'cruelly beat' at a meeting of the Independent Electors of Westminster at Vintners Hall, a meeting at which Sir John Cotton was present, but the Government took no action.

[1] *Murray of Broughton* 424, 445, 456–7; Ryder diary February 1747; *HC* ii 371; *H. Walpole Corresp.* xix 381.

[2] *HMC Polwarth* v 179; *H. Walpole Corresp.* xix 284; Add. 35588ff. 115, 253, 262, 264, 266, 270, 272, 282, 285; Add. 35589ff. 180, 185, 200.

Times were becoming more humane, and there was considerable public sympathy for the prisoners. Hogath in his *Four Stages of Cruelty* exposed practices regarded as normal in former ages. As strong a Whig as Horace Walpole was touched: 'The first appearance of the prisoners shocked me! Their behaviour melted me!' The spectacle of James Dawson, a young undergraduate from St. John's Cambridge, being half hanged, disembowelled, drawn, and quartered killed his sweetheart of shock, and produced public revulsion. Abroad, Voltaire denounced the barbarity of these executions as he was to expose those of Damiens, a madman who tried to murder Louis XV, and of Callas, a French Huguenot.[1]

There was considerable sympathy in England with the plight of the Scots. When it was proposed to offer the freedom of the City of London to Cumberland as the victor of Culloden, someone interjected 'Let it be the butchers', and that was that. In the past English Tories had been as suspicious of the Scots as the rest of England, but now they adopted the plaid as their emblem, a thing inconceivable a few years before. In May 1747 Ryder noted that by appearing 'publicly in body in Warwickshire, Leicestershire and Staffordshire with Scots plaids, waistcoats or other parts of their clothes of plaid', the Jacobites had shown 'they mean a signal to France of their readiness'. The principal targets of the Tory backlash were Lord Gower, who complained of being 'persecuted by the gout and Jacobitism', and the Duke of Bedford. Tory candidates were put up against all Lord Gower's candidates in Staffordshire. At the county election in 1747, Gower wrote to Newcastle that he found the voters in Lichfield—

insolent to a degree that you cannot easily conceive, and seem to me to be animated by the same Jacobite spirit that the mobs at Manchester and Ashbourn were, and can be quelled by no other means; I hope therefore you will order immediately some troops into that town or I think none of our friends can with safety attend the sessions, for they have threatened to pull down the gaol, if any of their accomplices are committed.

[1] *HMC 12th Rep. ix* 98; Badminton mss., Beaufort to Anne, Lady Coventry, Bath 21 December 1746; Howell, *State Trials* xviii. 335; Ryder diary 24 March 1747. *HC* ii 538, 545; Browne iii 337–9; Voltaire, *Siècle de Louis XV* (1826 ed.) i 267–72.

A friend of Gower's at Stafford, who had his house pulled down by the rioters, complained 'this popular rage and rebellious spirit has continued to show itself during the whole course of the county election'. These riots were said to have been stirred up by Sir James Harrington, an agent of Charles Edward's, presumably on his orders. Gower, whose interest in Staffordshire had been paramount, had lost most of it, and Pelham remarked that he owed what successes he did have 'almost entirely to the Whigs'.[1] At the Lichfield races that summer, Sir Watkin Williams Wynn organised Tory subscriptions in support of the expenses of Sir Walter Bagot, re-elected knight of the shire for Staffordshire, against the petition of Gower's candidate, Sir Richard Wrottesley, who had been defeated. But it was much more than that. Not only did Stafford-shire Tories turn up in force, but supporters were summoned 'from all parts of the kingdom'. In came 'the Burton mob, most of them in plaid waistcoats, plaid ribbon round their hats and some of them white cockades [the Stuart emblem]' led by Sir Charles Sedley, Member for Nottingham, and Sir Thomas Gresley, who succeeded Richard Leveson Gower as Member for Lichfield in 1753. 'About the same time came another party of the Birmingham people, most of them in the same dress, with Sir Lister Holte [M.P. Lichfield 1741], and some of the Warwickshire gentlemen. Sir Walter Bagot came in alone.' The Warwickshire contingent were said to have 'drunk the Pretender's health publicly in the streets, singing treasonable songs'. The Duke of Bedford was horsewhipped on the racecourse, and Gower's son, Lord Trentham, cudgelled. These events were recorded in the public prints, notably in *A sight of the Banging Bout at Lichfield*, and were said to have taken place to the tune of 'the King shall enjoy his own again'. Years later, Junius was reminding Bedford of 'those ridiculous scenes, by which in your earlier days you thought it an honour to be distinguished—the recorded stripes, the public infamy, your own sufferings'. A friend of Gower's wrote: 'You cannot conceive what noise the Lichfield hunting meeting makes in town, where people make no ceremony of treating the company as Jacobites . . .

[1] *H. Walpole Corresp.* xix 288; Ryder diary 16 May 1747; Woburn mss., Lord Gower to the Duke of Bedford, 3 Aug. 1747; Lord Anson to the Duke of Bed-ford, 21 June 1747; Add. 32712ff. 111, 117, 288; Stuart mss. 301/5; Chats-worth mss., Henry Pelham to Lord Hartington, June 1747.

His Majesty told me . . . he must and ought to consider that company as his declared enemies.' The persistence of Tory resentment against Gower was such that Dr Johnson, a Lichfield man, speaking of his dictionary, told Boswell: 'You know, Sir, Lord Gower forsook the old Jacobite interest. When I came to the word *Renegado*, after telling it meant "any one who deserts to the enemy, a revolter", I added "sometimes we say a Gower", but the printer struck it out.' A similar demonstration occurred at the Newton races in 1748, when Sir Thomas Egerton, the local Member of Parliament, and other members of the hunt were reported in the London press to have proclaimed the Pretender as James III wearing 'white cockades' and 'plaid waistcoats', and to have gone 'riding about to drink and to force others to drink treasonable healths'.[1]

The wearing of the plaid was even more prevalent in London. Alderman Benn, who had been present at the talks with Butler in 1743, and as lord mayor in 1747 had sent to Charles Edward in France a message of sympathy and support, had himself and fellow aldermen painted wearing plaid waistcoats. Nowhere was it more universal than among the Independent Electors of Westminster, satirised as *Jaco-Independo-Rebello-Plaido* in a public print. At the anniversary dinner of the Independent Electors in Vintners Hall in 1747, with the Earl of Lichfield, Lord Orrery, George Heathcote and Thomas Carew presiding as stewards, the *Gentleman's Magazine* reported:

> The following healths were drunk. The King (each man having a glass of water on the left hand, and waving the glass of wine over the water). The Prince, the Duke. Prosperity to the independent electors of Westminster. Prosperity to the city of London and the trade thereof. The Lord Mayor of London [Benn]. Success to the arms of Great Britain by sea and land . . . That the spirit of independency may diffuse itself throughout the nation . . . that the naturalization bill be kicked out of the House and the foreigners out of the kingdom.

The culmination of the campaign against Gower came at the Westminster by-election of 1749–50, stage-managed by Alexander

[1] Add. 32717f. 42; Lichfield mss. Hinton to Lord Anson 26 September 1747; *HC* i 317; ii 7, 321, 494; *Catalogue of Prints and Drawings in the British Museum*, satires 1734–50. No. 2863; *Letters of Junius* (1791 ed.) 103; *Boswell's Johnson*, ed. E. B. Hill, i 296.

Murray, who was influential amongst the Independent Electors and had been active at the 1747 Westminster election. Alexander Murray was an agent of Charles Edward's and never moved a step except upon his instructions. Unfortunately for us, the Prince's notes to Murray in the Stuart papers tell us where he was to go but not what he was to do, since Charles Edward did not believe in putting anything down in writing. Then, Horace Walpole wrote, 'the resentment of the Jacobites against Lord Gower for deserting their principles . . . appeared in the strongest colours'. Another Whig commented:

> There never was any election carried on with so much violence on both sides. The scandal and dirt flung upon Lord Gower's family and the Duke of Bedford's is shocking, and is enough to terrify anybody, and make them have some regard, great how they are how they exasperate an English mob.

Gower was put forward for the post of President of the Council but Pelham turned him down as 'broke in spirit and constitution'. Government supporters attacked the Independent Electors for—

> the earnestness with which they opposed all subscriptions or levies for suppressing the late rebellion: their suspected correspondencies, and the indecent (i.e. treasonable) healths so often proposed and so publicly drunk in their meetings and assemblies.

The retort was 'whose foot was in the stirrup in 1715?'—an allusion to Gower having gone to join the rebellion when Forster was defeated. The first petition of the Independent Electors against Lord Trentham's election drawn up by Alexander Murray said to be 'absolutely treason', was toned down by Sir John Cotton, who defended Murray's conduct at the scrutiny. Imprisoned in Newgate for contempt of the House of Commons, Murray was released by the sheriffs of London as soon as Parliament was prorogued, and he was taken through the streets of London in triumph 'with a standard before him whereon was inscribed "Murray and Liberty!" ' The printer of *The Case of Alexander Murray*, defending Murray and attacking the House of Commons as unrepresentative of the people, was acquitted by a Middlesex jury and given a public ovation on his release. The previous instance of an English jury deciding on a point of law as well as on a point of fact was the case of the Seven Bishops under James II.[1]

The Tory backlash took yet another form. In February 1748 there was a riot in Oxford with people in the streets shouting for King James. The vice-chancellor took no action, but the Government caught two undergraduates who were condemned to two years imprisonment for treason. Gower and Bedford 'pressed extremely for the trial of the vice-chancellor' too. Gower, Horace Walpole wrote,

> asked the attorney general his opinion, who told him the evidence did not appear strong enough. Lord Gower said, 'Mr. Attorney, you seem to be very lukewarm for your party'. He replied, 'My Lord, I never was lukewarm for my party, *nor ever was but of one party*'.

At the opening of the Radcliffe Library in 1749, with the Duke of Beaufort, Lord Oxford, Sir Walter Wagstaffe Bagot, and Sir Watkin Williams Wynn presiding as Radcliffe trustees, Dr King deplored the corruption of manners and the decay of the universities under the Hanoverians, punctuating his oration with the refrain '*redeat ille genius Britanniae*' which was universally interpreted as meaning the Young Pretender. The ministry began to consider action against Oxford, 'the sanctuary of disaffection', and were reported to be bringing in legislation to vest in the King the nomination of the chancellor of the university with a view of replacing the present chancellor Lord Arran (Ormonde's brother) by the Duke of Cumberland. The news, Carte wrote, brought all the Tories to town, 'which nothing else would'. Their numbers in Parliament had been decimated at the 1747 election in the aftermath of the rebellion, and they sought the help of Frederick, Prince of Wales, leader of the Whig opposition, who had been courting them without success since 1747 with offers to 'take away all proscriptions from any set of men whatever who are friends to the constitution' and other Tory points. Horace Walpole reported:

---

[1] Stuart mss. 288/172; Beaven ii 128, 292; *Catalogue of Prints and Drawings* No. 2856; *Gentleman's Magazine* 1747, 150; 1751, 283; *Malmesbury Letters* i 75. For Alexander Murray, see Andrew Lang, *Pickle the Spy*; Stuart mss. 269/191 and 288/172; *Westminster Elections 1741–51*; Walpole, *Memoirs of George II* i 13–17, 19–22, 25–31; *Parl. Hist.* xiv 893–4, 978, 1064–5; Howell, *State Trials* xviii 1203–30; *HC* i 77; ii 122.

This menace gave occasion to a meeting and union between the Prince's party and the Jacobites, which Lord Egmont has been labouring all the winter. They met at the St. Alban Tavern [the headquarters of the Loyal Brotherhood] near Pall Mall . . . 112 lords and commoners. The Duke of Beaufort opened the assembly with a panegyric on the stand that had been made this winter against so corrupt an Administration, and hoped it would continue, and desired harmony. Lord Egmont seconded this strongly . . . Lord Oxford spoke next, and then Potter with great humour and to the great abashment of the Jacobites, said he was very glad to see this union and from thence hoped, that if another attack like the last rebellion should be made on the royal family, they would all stand by them. No reply was made to this.

Carte wrote that they had agreed to 'a sort of coalition with Prince Frederick's party to stand by the University of Oxford, to join in opposing all unconstitutional points, to be under no obligation to visit Prince Frederick's court nor unite in other points'. Carte's patron, Sir John Cotton, however, who was much more a politician than the others, did sometimes go to Frederick's court. There was a meeting of the Cabinet to consider 'the reformation of the University of Oxford'. The solicitor general thought this 'might create a flame in the nation' and since Prince Frederick was defending the University could 'overthrow the present ministry'. Ryder, the attorney general, did not think 'materials in point of disloyalty could be found in evidence sufficient to charge the University', and it was agreed to drop the bill.[1] In its death throes, Jacobitism was bolder than it had been since the passing of the Riot Act in 1715, but the opportunity had gone for ever.

When Charles Edward returned to France after his escape and long wanderings through the Isles, he was welcomed as a hero. When he appeared in the royal box at the opera, the whole audience rose to clap. He was befriended by Montesquieu. He took his pick of the great ladies at Court who were in love with him. When Lord Cornbury went over to Paris, old loyalties were too

[1] *H. Walpole Corresp.* xx 6, 50, 137; *Gentleman's Magazine* 1749, 164–5; A. D. Godley, *Oxford in the Eighteenth Century* 257–8; *Bodleian Quarterly Record* i (1915) 165–72; Stuart mss. Box 1/299; *HC* i 75–6; Ryder diary 25 May 1749.

strong for him, and on his own admission he committed 'twenty extravagancies' in the Prince's company. But it did not last. Charles's friend the Marquis d'Argenson was disgraced for his too zealous championship of him and for involving France in diplomatic difficulties in trying to move heaven and earth at all European Courts to save the Jacobite prisoners. Although Maurice of Saxony defeated the Duke of Cumberland at Laffeldt, under the influence of Louis XV's new mistress Madame de Pompadour France concluded the peace of Aix-la-Chapelle in 1748 on terms which made *bête comme la paix* a French proverb. Charles Edward obstinately refused to leave France, or at least not to appear in public, and was arrested at the Paris opera. He had made himself popular with the French mob too, and there were riots in Paris after his arrest. Argenson, who was scandalised at his Government seizing like a criminal 'the son of the legitimate King of England', advised him never to go back to Rome. The English Government, resentful at not being able to keep him under observation, was sending spies all over Europe to try and track him down, as if he had been the Scarlet Pimpernel. Most of the time he was living privately in France with his uncle the Duc de Bouillon or elsewhere. Pelham wrote to Newcastle:

> If this young gentleman should declare himself a Protestant, and another [Frederick, Prince of Wales] should not act suitable to the great and good examples he has had before him, the Lord knows how matters may end.

Balhaldy, who was in London in the autumn of 1749, wrote to the Pretender that notwithstanding all the demonstrations in Staffordshire and elsewhere, the party was 'dispirited, frightened out of their wits at what had happened and without any trust or confidence in one another'. Charles Edward came over to London with Col. Brett in September 1750 without the Government finding out! He had a meeting with about fifty of his supporters, including the Duke of Beaufort and Lord Westmorland, and was received into the Anglican Church in Marylebone. He inspected the defences of the Tower of London and said one of the gates 'might be beaten down with a petard', but there was little to be done without an army. In 1752 there was a prospect of assistance from Prussia, Heathcote being one of the chief managers, but Frederick II was playing the Jacobite card only to bring pressure on the English Government.[1]

During the Seven Years War, Choiseul, the French foreign minister, formed a plan for a descent on Scotland on 1759. He did not consult the Pretender, although he had an inconclusive meeting with Charles Edward in France. Although he seriously considered a Stuart restoration, he could not have effected it in any case since the French fleet was annihilated by Admiral Hawke at Quiberon Bay. Under generals chosen by Madame de Pompadour, France went on to lose most of the battles of the Seven Years War. By this time most of the Tories realised that the cause they had supported for over forty years was hopeless. Charles Edward knew this too, and he had become an alcoholic, which led his last few supporters to abandon him. 'Jacobitism,' Horace Walpole wrote, 'the concealed mother' of Toryism was dead. The Tories could identify with the policies of the elder Pitt, and his use of sea-power, and could feel a genuine pride at England's victories. The accession of George III completed the task of national reconciliation. Once again, Tory peers were lords lieutenants of their counties and held places at Court. Once again, careers of every kind were open to Tories. By treating all Tories as his enemies, George I had made them Jacobites, and by continuing the same policy George II had kept them Jacobites. For the most part, the Whigs were very well pleased as it gave them a monopoly of office, but when it would have been politically more convenient to take the Tories in than keep them out—in 1721 and in 1742-4—they dared not risk sharing real political power with men they knew to be disaffected. The death of Jacobitism solved the problem of the proscription, and enabled George III to be the king of all his people.[2]

---

[1] Barbier ii 499, iv 45, 49, 57; Cornbury to Speaker Onslow 27 Jan. 1751, Royal Archives. There is in the Stuart papers a whole box of love letters from French ladies to the Prince; Argenson iv 308-25, 322-7; Andrew Lang, *Pickle the Spy* 178, 190, 213; Coxe, *Pelham* i 462; Stuart mss. 301/5; letter from Lord Stanhope to *The Times* 29 Dec. 1864; *HC* i 77.

[2] *Recueil des Instructions données aux ambassadeurs et ministres de France*, Angleterre, 1698-1791, ed. Vaucher, 370-1; *ex inf.* Professor Claude Nordmann; *HC* i 77-8; J. C. D. Clark, 'The decline of party', *English Historical Review* xciii (1978) 499-527; John Brooke, *George III* (1972 ed.) 25-207.

Appendix I

List of lords and country gentlemen in each county given to Butler in 1743

This list has been transcribed from the original (AEM & D. Ang. 76ff. 203–207). A copy (AEM & D. Ang. 82ff. 49–57) taken by a French Foreign Office clerk is imperfect as he could not cope with English names. Balhaldy sent a fair copy to James, the Old Pretender (Stuart mss. 253/51). Except where otherwise stated the information given in the notes is taken from Cokayne *Complete Baronetage* and *Complete Peerage* or from *The History of Parliament; the House of Commons 1715–1754* ed. Romney Sedgwick.

It is a list of persons expected to declare for a restoration, or more probably to declare for a free Parliament (as in 1660) to effect a restoration, in the event of a successful attempt by the French to restore the Stuarts. The majority are Tory peers or Tory M.P.s, or Opposition Whigs connected with the Whig lords who appear to have been a party to the bargain made with the Pretender to secure the fall of Walpole. A fair number are people in debt who would be expected to support a change of régime in exchange for rewards. Many are Roman Catholics, who though relatively few in numbers, held very large estates. Roman Catholics had not been active Jacobites since 1717 when at the request of the Duke of Norfolk they were allowed by the Pope to take the oaths to George I in order to avoid further penal taxation (Stuart mss. 206/2; Martin Haile, *James Edward Stuart, the Old Chevalier*, 232–4, 462–3), but they would naturally have welcomed a restoration. Another category is Roman Catholics who had conformed in order to get a career and might be expected to return to their former loyalties. Anglicans, who formed the bulk of Jacobites after 1717, with the exception of a few nonjurors, took the oaths under the assumption that oaths taken under duress were not binding, as the Cavaliers had done in the Civil Wars.

Septembre 1743. Etat des seigneurs ou gentilhommes qui ont le plus de crédit dans les differentes Provinces d'Angleterre et sur lesquels on peut compter.

Province de Bedford

Cette Province est entierement devouée au Roy legitime; le Duc de Bedford, le plus riche d'entre les sujets d'Angleterre en fond de terres, y a beaucoup de credit, et après ce duc, M. Charles Leigh qui a cinq mille livres sterling de rentes; M. Samuel Ongley qui en a six mille; le Chevalier Jean Chester qui en a cinq mille, le Chevalier Roger Bourgoyne qui en a quatre mille, et le Chevalier Boteler Chernock qui a pareillement quatre mille livres sterling de rentes, sont ceux auxquels les peuples de cette Province sont attachés.[1]

Province de Berks

Cette Province est sous la conduite de Mylords Craven, Willoughby de Brook, Stawell, Abingdon, et des Sieurs Howard Packer, Peniston Powney, Jean Blograve, et Guillaume Strode, gentilhommes dont le moins riche jouït de quatre mille livres sterling de rentes.[2]

Province de Buckingham

Cette Province est menée par le Duc de Bedford, les Mylords Chester-field, Orrery, Dormer, Masham et Bathurst, et par les Sieurs Greeville, Lowndes, Denton, Greenville, Marshal, Gore, Selby, et Fleetwood, tous gentilhommes qui y ont des terres considerables.[3]

Province de Cheshire

Cette Province suivra les mouvemens de Mylords Barrymore, Warrington et Mollineux, et du Chevalier Robert Grosvenor qui a vingt deux mille livres sterling de rentes, du Sieur Jean Crew, qui en a douze mille, et des Sieurs Charles Cholmondeley, Pierre Warburton, et les Messieurs de Leigh, tous gentilhommes très riches.[4]

Province de Cornouailles

Cette Province, distinguée par le grand nombre de mineurs qui s'y trouvent, a toujours eté attachée à son roi naturel; les Mylords Arundel de Trerice, Arundel de Wardour, et de Falmouth; les Chevaliers Guillaume Carew, Jean St. Aubin, et Guillaume Morris; les Sieurs Trelawney, Penton, Cooke, Lydell, Foster, Cotton, et Nugent, sont les plus accredités d'entre la noblesse qui y est nombreuse, brave et tres zelée.[5]

Province de Cambridge

l'Université de Cambridge, opposée à celle d'Oxford, a gâté une grande partie de cette Province, mais le Chevalier Jean Cotton, qui y a de gros biens, est en etat de la partager avec la Cour d'Hannover.[6]

Province de Cumberland

Cette Province est la plus pauvre et la plus corrompue de toute l'Angleterre; la plupart des terres y etoient autrefois du domaine de la couronne, et ont ete alienées depuis la Revolution à des gens qui craignent de les perdre par le rétablissement du Roi légitime; il n'y a dans toute la province que le Baron de Hilton et le Chevalier Haggerston sur lesquels on puisse compter avec assurance, quoiqu'il y ait plusieurs mécontens.[7]

Province de Derby

Le Duc de Rutland et Mylord Chesterfield, le Chevalier Nathaniel Curson, et Monsieur Jean Stanhope menent toute cette Province: le Chevalier Curson qui y possede douze mille livres sterling de rentes a dix mille mineurs sous ses ordres.[8]

Province de Devon

Cette Province est sous la conduite du Duc de Bedford, des Lords Clinton et Clifford, du Chevalier Courtenay qui y a dix mille livres sterling par an, du Sieur Fortescue qui y a six mille, du Chevalier Northcote qui en a cinq mille, et des Sieurs Sydenham et Littleton qui y ont aussi des terres considerables.[9]

Province de Dorset

Cette Province est menée par Mylord Dierhurst, par le Sieur George Chaffin, qui y possede quatre mille livres sterling de rentes, par le Sieur Pleydell qui en a cinq mille et par les Sieurs Brown, Richards et Pitts.[10]

Province de Durham

Cette petite Province a beaucoup de noblesse qui est generalement bien disposée; Mylord Falconberg, le Sieur Bowes qui y a dix mille livres sterling de revenu, et le Sieur Tempest sont à la tête de cette noblesse.[11]

Province d'Essex

Cette Province est sour la conduitte des Mylords Suffolk, Waldegrave, Petre, et Masham, des Chevaliers Abdy, Smith, et Long, des Sieurs Bramston, Smith, Grey, et Saville, tous gentilhommes de gros biens et d'un merite reconnu.[12]

Province de Gloucester

Cette Province est sous la conduite du Duc de Beaufort, des Mylords

Gainsborough, et Bathurst, des Sieurs Chester, Berkley, Benjamin Bathurst, Master, et Gage, gentilhommes dont le moindre a trois mille livres sterling de rentes.[13]

Province de Hereford

Cette Province est sous la conduite du Duc de Beaufort, des Mylords Oxford et Foley, des Sieurs Thomas Foley, Cornwall, Winford, Cope Hopton, de Monsieur Robert Harley, et les Messieurs Lowes. Le moins riche de ces gentilhommes a quatre mille livres sterling par an.[14]

Province de Hertford

Le Duc de Bridgewater, les Mylords Exeter et Stanhope, les Sieurs Gore, Houblon, et Stanley sont les conducteurs de cette Province qui est tres riche et bien peuplée.[15]

Province de Huntingdon

Les Mylords Sandwich et Rockingham, les Sieurs Mitchel et Fellows président dans cette Province, qui n'est point d'une grande étendue.[16]

Province de Kent

Cette Province, l'une des plus riches et des mieux peuplées de l'Angle-terre, qui s'étend sur la côte depuis Douvres jusqu'aux portes de Londres, est entirement sous la conduite des Mylords Westmorland, Thanet, Stanhope, Rockingham, Aylesford, Teynham, Guernsey, des Chevaliers Dering, Hales, et Dashwood, des Sieurs Dorill, Twisden, et Watson, gentilhommes qui y ont de gros biens.[17]

Province de Lancastre

Cette Province d'une grande étendue et ou il y a grand nombre de très anciennes maisons est absolument attachée au Roi legitime, sous la conduite des Mylords Derby, Barrymore, Petre, Chesterfield, Molineux, Strange, et des Sieurs Shuttleworth, Curzon, Fenwick, Fazakerly, Master, Lister, etc.[18]

Province de Leicester

Cette Province est menée par le Duc de Rutland, les Mylords Huntingdon et Stamford, le Chevalier Cave, les Sieurs Smith, Wigley et Wright.[19]

Province de Lincoln

Cette province suit les mouvements des Mylords Bristol et Haversham, des Sieurs Vyner, Wichcote, Mitchell et Proby.[20]

Province de Middlesex

Les gens de campagne, dans cette riche Province où la ville de Londres est située, ont toujours eu de bons sentiments; ils sont presque tous sous la conduite des Ducs de Somerset, de Beaufort, et de Bedford, de Mylord Burlington, et des Chevaliers Newdigate et Smithson, seigneurs ou gentilhommes qui y ont des fonds de terre tres considerables.[21]

Province de Monmouth

Cette Province est entierement soumise au Duc de Beaufort et à Mylord Noel Sommerset son frère.[22]

Province de Norfolk

La noblesse de cette Province est generalement attachee au Roy naturel, mais les dépenses excessives du Chevalier Walpole ont corrompu une grande partie du peuple. Le Duc de Norfolk, Mylord Andover, les Chevaliers Jerningham et Andrews, et le Sieur Woodhouse soutiennent le bon partie contre celui de Walpole.[23]

Province de Northampton

Cette Province est sous la conduite des Mylords Thanet et Rockingham, du Chevalier Edouard Isham, des Sieurs Cartwright, Parker, Shirley et Wortley: ce dernier jouit de vingt mille livres sterling de rentes.[24]

Province de Northumberland

Cette Province limitrophe de l'Ecosse abonde en maisons anciennes qui n'ont jamais eté perverties; presque toute la noblesse est unie avec les Mylords Derwentwater et Widrington, le Chevalier Swinburne, les Sieurs Fenwick et Blacket: ce dernier a sous ses ordres plusieurs milliers de ceux qui travaillent dans les mines de charbon de terre, qui se transporte par mer à Londres.[25]

Province de Nottingham

Cette Province est menee par le Duc de Norfolk, les Mylords Chesterfield, Middleton, et Trevor, les Sieurs Levinz et Warren.[26]

Province d'Oxford

Cette Province, fameuse par l'université qui a constament soutenu les principes de l'obeïssance passive, a une noblesse très nombreuse et très zélée; les Mylords Abingdon et Litchfield, le Chevalier Dashwood, le Docteur Butler, les Sieurs Rowney, Herbert, Dawkins, et Moore sont les plus distingués par leurs talens et leur credit.[27]

9

Province de Rutland

Les paysans de cette petite Province sont presque tous sous les ordres des Mylords Gainsborough et Westmorland, et du Sieur Jacques Noel. Les villes y sont entierement gatées. [28]

Province de Shropshire

Cette Province est presque unanimement Jacobite; elle est sous la conduite des Chevaliers Astley et Corbet, des Messieurs de la Maison de Kynaston et du Sieur Lister. [29]

Province de Somerset

Cette Province d'un étendue considerable renferme une noblesse generalement zelée pour le Roy le gitime; le Duc de Beaufort, les Mylords Orrery, Clifford, et Stawell, le Chevalier Chapman, les Sieurs Portman, Prouze, Houblon, Buck, Carey, Dodington et Harvey y ont le plus de biens et de credit. [30]

Province de Southampton

Cette Province plus riche qu'étendue est generalement gatée; néanmoins les Mylords Shaftsbury et Dormer, le Chevalier Barington, et les Sieurs Delmé et Gibbon, tous zélés Jacobites, y ont beaucoup de credit. [31]

Province de Stafford

Cette Province situee à peu pres au milieu de l'Angleterre, et l'une des plus riches qu'il y ait, est unanimement attachée au Roy legitime; les Mylords Shrewsbury, Berkshire, Audley, Stourton, Gower, Ward, Stamford, Leigh, Chetwind, les Chevaliers Wagstaffe Baggot, Lister Holt, Guillaume Fowler, Guillaume Woosley, Guillaume Ridgley, les Sieurs Lewison Gore, Baptist Gore, Venables Vernon, et Wilbraham, le Colonel Lane et plusieurs autres qui y possedent des terres trés considerables, sont d'une fidelité à toute épreuve. C'étoit aux courses de chevaux qui se sont faites à Litchfield, ville de cette Province que Monsieur Butler a eu le plaisir de voir une assemblée de plus de trois cent seigneurs ou gentilhommes, dont le moins riche a près de quatre mille livres sterling par an, qui ont tous declaré qu'ils sont prêts à suivre les mouvemens de Mylord Barrymore pour parvenir au retablissement de leur Roi naturel. [32]

Province de Suffolk

Cette Province est menée par les Mylords Suffolk et Bristol, par le Chevalier Cordel Firebrace, qui y jouït de six mille livres sterling par an, par le Sieur Affleck, qui en possede quatre mille, et par le Chevalier Thomas Hanmer qui en a dix mille. [33]

Province de Surrey

La plûpart des terres de cette Province ont eté acquises par des agioteurs et autres partisans du Gouvernement, ce qui fait que les ministres y emportent tout: il y a cependant des seigneurs d'un grand merite qui y ont des terres, entre autres Mylord Butler de Weston frère du Duc d'Ormond, les Mylords Aylesford, St. Jean, et Montjoy, et les Sieurs Thrale, Newland, Harvey, Scawen, et Woodroffe sont aussi des gentilhommes incorruptibles.[34]

Province de Sussex

Le Gouvernement a beaucoup de partisans dans cette Province qui est une des plus considerables du Royaume, mais les plus anciennes maisons et ceux qui sont les plus riches en fonds de terres sont invariablement attaches au Roy legitime; entre autres nous sommes assurés des Ducs de Norfolk et de Somerset qui y font souvent leur residence, des Mylords Derby, Montacute, Thanet et Caryll, des Chevaliers Goring, Fag et Peachy, des Sieurs Campion, Kemp, Webster, et Richard Caryll, qui y ont tous de gros biens.[35]

Province de Warwick

Cette Province qui est au centre du Royaume a toujours eté des mieux disposée; elle est menée par les Mylords Westmorland, Denbigh, Northampton, Aylesford, Hereford, Willoughby de Brook, Brook, Craven, Middleton; par les Chevaliers Throgmorton et Mordaunt; par les Sieurs Edouard Digby, Sheldon, Carrington, Berkley, Grove, Farmer, Perkins, et autres, dont plusieurs ont au moins dix mille livres sterling de rentes.[36]

Province de Westmorland

Cette Province est la moins bien cultivée d'Angleterre; l'aliénation des domaines du Roy y a corrompu environ la moitié des habitans: Le Chevalier Musgrave est le seul homme de condition auquel nous nous fions dans ces cantons.[37]

Province de Wilts

Cette Province, quoique peu etendue est très bien cultivée et tres riche; il y a une nombreuse noblesse dont la plûpart sont des personnes affidées; Le Duc de Somerset, les Mylords Berkshire, Arundel de Wardour, Craven, et St. Jean; les Chevaliers Robert Long, Jacob Bouverie, Edouard Seymour, Edouard Turner, les Sieurs Popham, Greenville. Pitt, Thursby, Neale, et Crawley y sont très distingués tant par leurs gros biens que par l'ardeur de leur zèle.[38]

Province de Worcester

La ville de Worcester tient encoure du levain de Cromwell, mais la Province est très bien disposée; elle suit les mouvemens des Mylords Shrewsbury, Coventry, et Foley; des Sieurs Lechemere, Pitt, et Foley, tous gentilhommes très riches.[39]

Province de York

Cette Province, la plus grande de l'Angleterre, est un peu gatée du coté de Hull, mais la noblesse est generalement attachée a son souverain legitime, et les gens de campagne y sont presque tous prêts à suivre le Duc de Norfolk, les Mylords Aylesbury, Shrewsbury, Burlington, Carlisle, Gower, Langdale, Abingdon; des Chevaliers Miles Stapleton et Henry Slingsby; des Sieurs George Fox, Aislaby, Berkley et Charles Pelham, gentilhommes dont le moindre a quatre mille livres sterling en fond de terre.[40]

Principauté de Galles

Les douze Provinces de la Principauté de Galles sont entierement soumises aux Ducs de Beaufort et de Powis, au Mylord Bulkely, au Chevalier Watkin Williams et a ceux qui sont unis avec ces seigneurs, qui sont tous engagés a se tenir prêts à monter à cheval au premier signal que Mylord Barrymore leur donnera.[41]

La ville de Londres et de Westminster

[The first part has been omitted as it duplicates the account of the City of London given in Appendix II. The text then goes on:]

Il est visible par ce detail qu'on peut juger sainement du penchant et des sentimens des citoyens de Londres par les choix qu'ils font de leur mayors, sheriffs et membres du Parlement: choix qui sont éclatants et dont l'observation ne peut échapper à personne; mais pour mettre la disposition de cette grande ville dans une evidence entière, l'on a examiné les principes et la conduite de chacun de deux cent trente six, qui composent actuellement le commun conseil, et l'on a trouvé qu'il y en a actuellement cent quatre vingt six qui sont jacobites zélés: On a donne une liste a Monsieur Butler en luy indiquant les moyens de la verifier par lui même, ce qu'il a pris la peine a faire avec une exactitude scrupuleuse et a eu le plaisir d'être temoin des voeux qu'ils font pour le retablissement de leur Roy legitime et de l'ardeur avec laquelle ils aspirent après le secours du Roy tres Chretien pour y parvenir.

Il seroit inutile d'entrer dans le detail des autres grandes villes du royaume dont la plupart suivent l'example et les mouvements de celle de Londres dans les conjonctures importantes. C'est ainsi que dans le tems des dernières elections des membres du Parlement, elles adopterent presque unanimement les instructions que la ville de Londres a juge a propos de donner à ses députés. Mais la conduite de la ville de Westminster, qui touche à Londres et dans laquelle le Roy fait séjour est tres digne de remarque. Cette ville a droit de choisir deux membres du Parlement, et comme ce choix devoit se faire sous les yeux de la cour et de tous les ministres étrangers qui y étoient, Walpole mit en usage toute sorte de pratiques, et eut enfin recours à la violence pour faire tomber le choix sur deux de ses creatures. Les habitants indignés de ce procéde se réunisent avec une ardeur incroyable, et firent choix de deux hommes dont l'un est jacobite zelé et l'autre un mécontent que Walpole s'etoit vante d'exclure de toute seance au Parlement.[42] Les habitans ont prouve dans cette occasion, que tous les tresors dont ce ministre avoit la disposition etoient incapables de les corrompre. Monsieur Butler a entendu de la bouche de celui qui a mene toute l'opposition de Westminster a la cour presente ne provient que de leur zèle pour leur Roy legitime et naturel.

FOOTNOTES TO APPENDIX I

Bedford

[1] Bedford, 4th Duke of (1710–1771). (See pp. 44–5, and under Bucks, Devon and Middlesex.

Leigh, Hon. Charles (*c.* 1685–1749), of Leighton Buzzard, Beds. M.P. Warwick 13 Dec. 1710–1713, Higham Ferrers 12 Mar. 1714–1722, Bedfordshire 1722–1727, 16 Feb. 1733–1734. Tory.

Ongley, Samuel (1697–1747), of Old Warden, Beds. M.P. New Shoreham 29 Jan. 1729–1734, Bedford 1734–15 June 1747. Tory.

Chester, Sir John, 6th Bt. (1693–1748), of Chicheley, Bucks and Lidlington, Beds. M.P. Bedfordshire 1741–1747. Tory.

Burgoyne, Sir Roger, 6th Bt. (1710–1780), of Sutton, Beds. M.P. Bedfordshire 26 Feb. 1735–1747. A Whig who went into opposition in 1739 and came back to the Government side in Dec. 1744.

Chernock, Sir Boteler, 4th Bt. (1696–1756), of Holcot, Beds. M.P. Bedford 24 Nov. 1740–1747. Tory.

Berks

[2] Craven, Fulwar, 4th Baron (d. 1764). (See under Warwickshire and Wilts.) Tory.

Willoughby de Broke, Richard Verney, 13th Lord (1693–1752). (See under Warwickshire.) Tory.

Stawell, Edward, 4th Baron (1685–1755). (See under Somerset.) A Tory and a poor lord. (See Holmes, *British Politics*, 391–2.)

Abingdon, Willoughby Bertie, 3rd Earl of (1692–1760). (See under

Oxfordshire and Yorkshire.) M.P. Westbury 28 March–1 June 1715. Tory. Refused Association in 1745.

Packer, Winchcomb Howard (1702–1746), of Donnington and Shellingford, Berks. M.P. Berkshire 5 May 1731–21 Aug. 1746. Tory.

Powney, Peniston (c. 1699–1757) of Ives Place, Bucks. M.P. Berkshire 5 Dec. 1739–8 Mar. 1757. Tory.

Blagrave, John (1713–1787), of Southcot, nr. Reading, Berks. M.P. Reading 6 Dec. 1739–1747. Tory.

Strode, William (c. 1712–1755), of Ponsbourne, Herts and Mapledurham, Oxon. M.P. Reading 26 Nov. 1740–17 Feb. 1741, 1741–1747, 1754–29 Apr. 1755. Tory.

Buckingham

[3] Chesterfield, Philip Dormer Stanhope, 4th Earl of (1694–1773). (See pp. 27–8 and under Derbyshire, Lancs and Notts.) M.P. St. Germans 3 May 1715–1722, Lostwithiel 1722–May 1723.

Orrery, John Boyle, 5th Earl of [1] (1707–1762). (See pp. 42, 46 and under Somerset.)

Dormer, Charles, 6th Baron (d. 1761). (See under Hampshire.) Roman Catholic priest. Arrested on suspicion of favouring Charles Edward in 1745, he is said to have secured his release by claiming his peerage (Kirk, 65).

Masham, Samuel, 1st Baron (d. 1758). (See under Essex.) M.P. Ilchester 1710–1711, New Windsor May–Dec. 1711. Tory. Husband of Queen Anne's favourite.

Bathurst, Allen, 1st Baron (1684–1775). (See pp. 12, 44 and under Glos.) M.P. Cirencester 1705–1712. Tory.

Greville, Fulke (1717–c. 1805), of Wilbury, Wilts. M.P. Monmouth 1747–1754. Tory and a relation of the Duke of Beaufort. His family had lands in the county.

Lowndes, Richard (c. 1707–1775), of Winslow, Bucks. M.P. Buckinghamshire 1741–1774. Tory.

Denton, George (c. 1703–1757), of Wardington, Oxon and Hillesden, Bucks. M.P. Buckingham 20 Feb. 1728–1747. Opposition Whig connected with Cobham.

Grenville, George (1712–1770). M.P. Buckingham 1741–13 Nov. 1770. Opposition Whig and one of the Cobham cubs.

Marshall, Henry (1688–1754), of St. Mary at Hill, London and Theddlethorpe, Lincs. M.P. Amersham 1734–2 Feb. 1754. Tory. Alderman and lord mayor of London. Supported London address upon the rebellion in 1745.

Gore, Thomas (c. 1694–1777), of the Inner Temple and Dunstan Park, Berks. (See p. 76.) M.P. Cricklade 1722–1727, Amersham 17 Feb. 1735–1746. Portsmouth 3 Mar. 1746–1747, Bedford 1747–1754, Cricklade 1754–1768, Tory connected with Gower.

Selby, Thomas James (d. 1772), of Whaddon Hall, Bucks. Tory and a friend of Lowndes (Lipscomb, iii. 497).

Fleetwood, John (c. 1685–1745), Missenden, Bucks. M.P. Buckinghamshire 1713–1722. Tory. Died before the rebellion.

Cheshire

[4] Barry, James, 4th Earl of Barrymore [1] (1667–1748). (See pp 42, 60–1 and under Lancs.) M.P. Stockbridge 1710–1713, 30 Apr. 1714–1715, Wigan 1715–1727, 1734–1747.

Warrington, George Booth, 2nd Earl of (1675–1758). Whig. A poor lord (Namier, *Structure of Politics*, 222, 223). He was reported to have armed his tenants in October 1745 but took no active part against the rebels (Jarvis ii 16).

Molyneux, Caryll, 6th Visct. (1683–1745). (See under Lancs.) Roman Catholic with large estates in and around Liverpool (See G. Molineux, *Molineux Family* and Rev. E. Horley, *Sefton*).

Grosvenor, Sir Robert, 6th Bt. (1695–1755), of Eaton Hall, Cheshire. (See pp. 20, 91.) M.P. Chester 24 Jan. 1733–1 Aug. 1755. Tory. Took subscriptions in 1745 (Jarvis ii 16).

Crewe, John (1681–1749), of Madeley, Staffs, and Crewe Hall, Cheshire. M.P. Newcastle-under-Lyme 1703–1705, Cheshire 1705–1710, 1722–1727. Tory. He stood bail for £15,000 for Lord Barrymore in 1744 (Northumberland mss., Lady Hertford to Lord Beauchamp, 2 Apr. 1744).

Cholmondeley, Charles (1685–1756), of Vale Royal, Cheshire. M.P. Cheshire 1710–1715, 1722–30 March 1756. Tory. He was closely connected with Lord Barrymore (Ormerod i 557).

Warburton, Peter (1708–1774), of Turner's Hill, Herts. Tory. He succeeded his uncle Sir George Warburton, 3rd Bt., M.P. as 4th Bt. and at Warburton and Arley, Cheshire 29 June 1743 (Ormerod i 575).

Legh, Peter (1669–1744), of Lyme, Cheshire. M.P. Newton 1685–1687. Nonjuror and proprietor of the borough of Wigan. Like Barrymore and Cholmondeley he decided against joining the '15 after the arrest of the West Country Jacobites (Ormerod i 557). (See Lady Newton.)

Legh, Peter (1707–1792), of Bank Hall, Cheshire. Nephew of the above and M.P. Newton 15 Dec. 1743–1774. Tory.

Cornwall

[5] Arundel, John, 4th Baron Arundel of Trerice (1701–1768). Roman Catholic.

Arundell, Henry, 6th Baron Arundell of Wardour (1694–1746). (See under Wilts.) Wealthy Roman Catholic.

Boscawen, Hugh, 2nd Visct. Falmouth (1707–1782). M.P. Truro 1727–1734. Opposition Whig who went over to the Government in 1744.

Carew, Sir William, 5th Bt. (1689–1744), of Antony, Cornwall. (See pp. 41, 43.) M.P. Saltash 17 Jan. 1711–1713, Cornwall 1713–8 Mar. 1744. Tory.

St. Aubyn, Sir John, 3rd Bt. (*c.* 1702–1744), of Clowance, and St. Michael's Mount, Cornwall. (See pp. 43, 47.) M.P. Cornwall 1722–15 Aug. 1744. Tory.

Morice, Sir William, 3rd Bt. (*c.* 1707–1750), of Werrington, Devon. M.P. Newport 1727–1734, Launceston 1734–17 Jan. 1750. Tory.

Trelawny, John (1691–1756), of Trelawne, nr. Looe, Cornwall. M.P. West Looe 20 Apr. 1713–1715, Liskeard 1715–1722, West Looe 1722–1727, East Looe 1727–1734. Tory under Queen Anne who went over to the Whigs under the Hanoverians. He was in financial trouble.

Penton, Henry (*c.* 1705–1762), of Eastgate House, Winchester, Hants. M.P. Tregony 1734–1747, Winchester 1747–1761. Whig and Government supporter. Very little is known about his connections.

Cooke, George (*c.* 1705–1768), of Bellamond or Bellackets in Harefield, Mdx. M.P. Tregony 28 Jan. 1742–1747, Middlesex 8 Mar. 1750–5 June 1768. Returned for Tregony by 2nd Visct. Falmouth. Called 'a pompous Jacobite' by Horace Walpole.

Liddell, Richard (*c.* 1694–1746), of Wakehurst Place, Sussex. M.P. Bossiney 12 May–11 Dec. 1741, 18 Mar. 1742–22 June 1746. Opposition Whig connected with Chesterfield who chose him as his chief secretary when lord lieutenant of Ireland.

Foster, Thomas (*c.* 1720–1765), of Elim, Jamaica, and Egham House, Surrey. M.P. Bossiney 12 May–11 Dec. 1741, 18 Mar. 1742–1747, Dorchester 1761–20 Oct. 1765. Opposition Whig.

Cotton, John Hynde (*c.* 1717–1795). M.P. St. Germans 1741–1747, Marlborough 18 Feb. 1752–1761, Cambridgeshire 22 Mar. 1764–1780. Tory. Son of Sir John Hynde Cotton.

Nugent, Robert (1709–1788), of Gosfield, Essex. M.P. St. Mawes 1741–1754, Bristol 1754–1774, St. Mawes 1774–June 1784. Irish Roman Catholic who conformed and became a protégé of Chesterfield.

Cambridge

[6] Cotton, Sir John Hynde, 3rd Bt. (*c.* 1688–1752), of Madingley Hall, Cambs. (See pp. 39–42.) M.P. Cambridge 1708–1722, Cambridgeshire 1722–1727, Cambridge 1727–1741, Marlborough 1741–4 Feb. 1752.

Cumberland

[7] Hylton, John (1699–1746), of Hylton Castle, co. Dur. One of small group of ancient families holding feudal baronies. M.P. Carlisle 1727–1741, 26 Jan. 1742–25 Sept. 1746. Tory. Stood bail for a rebel in 1746 (Mounsey 179–80).

Haggerston, Sir Carnaby, 3rd Bt. (*c.* 1700–1756), of Haggerston Castle, Northumb. Roman Catholic (*Northumberland Co. History* ii 263, 265).

Derby

[8] Rutland, John Manners, 3rd Duke of (1696–1779). (See under Leicestershire.) M.P. Rutland 21 Jan. 1719–22 Feb. 1721. Opposition Whig. Raised a regiment of foot against rebellion in 1745. Henry Pelham described him on 19 Nov. 1745 as 'frightened for his money' (to Duke of Devonshire, Chatsworth mss.), not active against rebellion until after retreat from Derby.

Curzon, Sir Nathaniel, 4th Bt. (*c.* 1676–1758), of Kedleston, Derbs. M.P. Derby 25 Apr. 1713–1715, Clitheroe 1722–1727, Derbyshire 1727–1754. Tory. His attitude to the rebels while he was at Kedleston in December 1745 was equivocal (Simpson 276–7).

Stanhope, Hon. John (1705–1748), of Blackheath, Kent. M.P. Nottingham 1727–1734, Derby 13 March 1736–14 Dec. 1748. Opposition Whig and brother of Chesterfield.

Devon

[9] Clinton, Hugh Fortescue, 1st Baron (1696–1751). Opposition Whig. Went to France with Lord Barrymore in 1740 (Stuart mss. 222/109A).

Clifford, Hugh, 4th Baron (1726–1783). (See under Somerset.) Grandson of Charles II's lord treasurer. Roman Catholic who became brother-in-law of 3rd Earl of Lichfield.

Courtenay, Sir William, 3rd Bt. (1710–1762), of Powderham Castle, Devon. M.P. Honiton 1734–1741, Devon 1741–6 May 1762. Tory.

Fortescue, Theophilus (*c.* 1707–1746), of Castle Hill, Filleigh, nr. Barnstaple, Devon. M.P. Barnstaple 1727–1741, Devon 1741–13 Mar. 1746. Opposition Whig and younger brother of Lord Clinton.

Northcote, Sir Henry, 5th Bt. (1710–1743), of Hayne and the Pynes, nr. Exeter, Devon. M.P. Exeter 11 Mar. 1735–24 May 1743. Tory.

Sydenham, Humphrey (1694–1757), of Combe, nr. Dulverton, Somerset and Nutcombe, Devon. M.P. Exeter 1741–1754. Tory.

Lyttelton, George (1709–1773), of Hagley Hall, Worcs. M.P. Okehampton 28 Mar. 1735–18 Nov. 1756. Opposition Whig and a Cobham cub.

Dorset

[10] Deerhurst, Thomas Henry Coventry, Visct. (1721–1744). M.P. Bridport 2 Apr. 1742–20 May 1744. Opposition Whig.

Chaffin, George (1689–1766), of Chettle, Dorset. M.P. Dorset 1713–1754. Tory.

Pleydell, Edmund Morton (*c.* 1693–1754), of Milborne St. Andrew, Dorset. M.P. Dorchester 1722–13 Feb. 1723, Dorset 1727–1747. Tory.

Browne, John (1696–1750), of Forston in Charminster, Devon. M.P. Dorchester 1727–25 Apr. 1750. Tory.

Richards, George (d. 1746), of Long Bredy, nr. Bridport, Dorset. M.P. Bridport 1741–25 Nov. 1746. Opposition Whig.

Pitt, George (aft. 1691–1745), of Shroton, Dorset and Strathfieldsaye, Hants. M.P. Wareham 18 Apr. 1715–1722, Dorset 25 Jan.–5 Aug. 1727. Tory.

Durham

[11] Fauconberg, Thomas Belasyse, 4th Visct. (1699–1774). Roman Catholic who conformed. Whig.

Bowes, George (1701–1760), of Streatlam Castle, co. Dur. M.P. co. Durham 1727–17 Sept. 1760. Opposition Whig. Active in raising forces against rebels in 1745.

Tempest, John (1710–1776), of Sherburn, nr. Durham. M.P. Durham 23 Apr. 1742–1768. Tory.

Essex

[12] Suffolk, Henry Howard, 10th Earl of (1707–1745). (See under Suffolk.) M.P. Bere Alston 2 Mar. 1728–28 Sept. 1733. Opposition Whig.

Waldegrave, James, 2nd Earl (1715–1763). Of a Jacobite Roman Catholic family. Conformed and served as ambassador at Paris 1730–1740. Friend of Cobham, *Lyttelton Memoirs* i 203).

Petre, Robert Edward, 9th Baron (1742–1801). (See under Lancs.) An infant whose vast estates were administered by his mother Lady Petre. His house at Walmesley was searched for arms in 1745 (Aveling 262).

Abdy, Sir Robert, 3rd Bt. (1688–1748), of Albyns, Essex. (See pp. 38, 42.) M.P. Essex 1727–27 Aug. 1748. Tory.

Smith, Sir Edward, 3rd Bt. (1686–1744), of Hill Hall, Essex. (See pp. 43, 78.)

Long, Sir Robert, 6th Bt. (c. 1705–1767), of Draycot Cerne, Wilts. (See under Wilts.) M.P. Wootton Bassett 1734–1741, Wiltshire 1741–1767. Tory. Acquired large Essex estates by marriage.

Bramston, Thomas (c. 1690–1765), of Skreens, nr. Maldon, Essex. (See pp. 43, 54). M.P. Maldon 28 Jan. 1712–1734, Essex 1734–1747. Tory.

Smith, Hugh (c. 1673–1745), of South Weald, Essex. Tory whose daughter married a younger son of Lord Barrymore (Morant i 119).

Gray, Charles (1696–1782), of Holly Trees, Colchester. (See p. 43.) M.P. Colchester 26 Feb. 1742–13 Mar. 1755, 1761–1780. Tory.

Savill, Samuel (c. 1700–1763), of Colchester and Stisted Hall, Essex. (See p. 43.) M.P. Colchester 26 Feb. 1742–1747. Tory.

Gloucester

[13] Beaufort, Henry Somerset, 3rd Duke of (1707–1745). (See pp. 38, 46 and under Herefordshire, Middlesex, Monmouthshire, Somerset, Wales.) Tory.

Gainsborough, Baptist Noel, 4th Earl of (1708–1751). (See under Rutland.) Tory.

Chester, Thomas (1696–1763), of Almondsbury and Knole nr. Bristol. M.P. Gloucester 1727–16 Feb. 1728, Gloucestershire 1734–1 Oct. 1763. Tory.

Berkeley, Norborne (c. 1717–1770), of Stoke Gifford, Glos. M.P. Gloucestershire 1741–Apr. 1763. Tory and brother-in-law of Lord Noel Somerset.

Bathurst, Hon. Benjamin (1711–1767), of Siddington, nr. Cirencester, Glos. M.P. Gloucestershire 1734–1741, Cirencester 1754–1761. Tory and son of Lord Bathurst.

Master, Thomas (1690–1770), of the Abbey, Cirencester, Glos. M.P. Cirencester 23 Jan. 1712–1747. Tory.

Gage, Thomas (c. 1695–1754), of High Meadow, Glos. M.P. Minehead 11 Apr.–23 May 1717, Tewkesbury 25 Oct. 1721–1754. Roman Catholic who conformed. Opposition Whig.

Hereford

[14] Oxford, Edward Harley, 3rd Earl of (c. 1699–1755). (See pp. 74–5.) M.P. Herefordshire 1727–16 June 1741. Tory.

Foley, Thomas, 2nd Baron (c. 1703–1776). (See under Worcs and p. 105.) Tory.

Foley, Thomas (c. 1695–1749), of Stoke Edith Court, Herefs. M.P. Hereford 1734–1741, Herefordshire 6 Jan. 1742–1747. Tory.

Cornewall, Velters (c. 1697–1768), of Moccas Court, Herefs. M.P. Herefordshire 1722–3 Apr. 1768. Tory.

Winford, Thomas Geers (c. 1697–1753), of Bridge Sollers nr. Hereford. M.P. Hereford 1727–1734, 1741–1747, Worcester 1747–11 Feb. 1748. Tory.

Cope, Edward Hopton (*c.* 1708–1754), of Canon Frome, nr. Hereford. M.P. Hereford 1741–1747. Tory.

Harley, Robert (*c.* 1706–1774). M.P. Leominster 1734–1741, 29 Mar. 1742–1747, Droitwich 1754–15 Mar. 1774. Tory.

Lowes, Messrs. Probably members of the family of Lowe of All Saints, Hereford.

Hertford

[15] Bridgwater, Scroop Egerton, 1st Duke of (1681–1745). Brother-in-law of Duke of Bedford. Opposition Whig connected with Chesterfield (*Lyttelton Memoirs* i 11).

Exeter, Brownlow Cecil, 8th Earl of (1701–1754). M.P. Stamford 24 Mar.–9 Apr. 1722. Tory.

Stanhope, Philip Stanhope, 2nd Earl (1714–1786). (See under Kent.) Opposition Whig and kinsman of Chesterfield.

Gore, Charles (*c.* 1711–1768), of Tring, Herts. (See p. 76.) M.P. Cricklade 21 Nov. 1739–1741, Hertfordshire 1741–1761, Tiverton 14 May 1762–1768. Tory.

Houblon, Jacob (1710–1770), of Hallingbury, Essex. (See under Somerset.) M.P. Colchester 20 Mar. 1735–1741, Hertfordshire 1741–1747, 1761–1768. Tory and son-in-law of Sir John Hynde Cotton.

Stanley, Hans (1721–1780), of Paultons, nr. Romsey, Hants. M.P. St. Albans 11 Feb. 1743–1747, Southampton 1754–12 Jan. 1780. Opposition Whig.

Huntingdon

[16] Sandwich, John Montagu, 4th Earl of (1718–1792). Whig; grandson of Jacobite Lady Sandwich.

Rockingham, Lewis Watson, 2nd Earl of (1714–1745). (See under Kent and Northants.) Opposition Whig.

Mitchell, William (*c.* 1703–1745), of Hemingford Grey, Hunts. M.P. Huntingdonshire 1741–15 Sept. 1745. Whig of Scottish origin, usually Government supporter.

Fellowes, Coulson (1696–1769), of Ramsey Abbey, Hunts. M.P. Huntingdonshire 1741–1761. Opposition Whig connected with Sandwich.

Kent

[17] Westmorland, John Fane, 7th Earl of (1686–1762). (See under Rutland and Warwickshire and pp. 46, 58). M.P. Hythe 1708–27 Jan. 1711, Kent 28 Sept. 1715–1722, Buckingham 1 Mar. 1727–1734. Tory.

Thanet, Sackville Tufton, 7th Earl of (1688–1753). (See under Northants and Sussex.) M.P. Appleby 1722–30 July 1739. In September 1745 gave assurances of loyalty to George II, but tried to persuade him to call a free Parliament (Add. 47098B f. 11 and *Marchmont Papers* ii 124). Tory.

Aylesford, Heneage Finch, 2nd Earl of (*c.* 1683–1757). (See under Surrey and Warwks.) M.P. Maidstone 3 Nov. 1704–1705, Surrey 1710–22 July 1719. Tory.

Teynham, Henry Roper, 10th Baron (1708–1781). Roman Catholic.

Guernsey, Heneage Finch, Lord (1715–1777). M.P. Leicestershire 20 Dec. 1739–1741, Maidstone 1741–1747, 1754–29 June 1757. Tory; son of Lord Aylesford.

Dering, Sir Edward, 5th Bt. (1705–1762), of Surrenden Dering, Kent. M.P. Kent 2 Apr. 1733–1754. Tory.

Hales, Sir Thomas, 2nd Bt. (1666–1748), of Bekesbourne, nr. Canterbury, Kent. M.P. Kent 1701–1705, Canterbury 1715–1734, 11 Apr. 1735–1741, 23 Jan. 1746–1747. Whig belonging to a junior branch of a Jacobite family.

Dashwood, Sir Francis, 2nd Bt. (1708–1781), of West Wycombe, Bucks. M.P. New Romney 1741–1761, Weymouth and Melcombe Regis 1761–19 Apr. 1763. Opposition Whig; nephew of Lord Westmorland.

Darell, John (d. 1761), of Scotney Castle and Calehill, Kent (Hasted, *Kent*, ii 318) Roman Catholic.

Twisden, Mr. Probably one of brothers of Sir Roger Twisden, 5th Bt. of Bradbourne, Kent (see Sir J. R. Twisden, *Twisden Family*).

Watson, Hon. Thomas (1715–1746). M.P. Canterbury 1741–4 Dec. 1745. Opposition Whig and brother of 3rd Earl of Rockingham.

Lancaster
[18] Derby, Edward Stanley, 11th Earl of (1689–1776). (See p. 89 and under Sussex.) M.P. Lancashire 1727–13 Apr. 1736. Opposition Whig.

Strange, James Stanley, Lord (1717–1771). M.P. Lancashire 1741–1 June 1771. Eldest son of Lord Derby. Independent Whig 'of a party by himself', usually voting with the Tories. Referred to the Stuarts as 'that rascally family', yet sat in on meetings of Independent Electors of Westminster while treasonable healths were being drunk (*Gentleman's Magazine* 1747, p. 150).

Shuttleworth, Richard (1683–1748), of Gawthorpe Hall, Lancs. M.P. Lancashire 1705–22 Dec. 1749. Regarded as 'one of the strongest Jacobites in all England'. Stood bail for £15,000 for Lord Barrymore in 1744 (Northumberland mss., Lady Hertford to Lord Beauchamp, 2 April 1744).

Curzon, William (*c.* 1681–1749), of the Inner Temple. (See under Derbyshire.) M.P. Clitheroe 1734–1747. Tory; brother of Sir Nathaniel Curzon.

Fenwick, Robert (1688–1750), of Burrow Hall, Lancs. M.P. Lancaster 1734–1747. Independent Whig; had Jacobite kinsmen.

Fazakerley, Nicholas (*c.* 1685–1767), of Prescot, Lands. (See p. 67.) M.P. Preston 24 Jan. 1732–Feb. 1767. Tory.

Master, Legh (*c.* 1694–1750), of New Hall, Ashton in Makerfield, Lancs. M.P. Newton 1727–1747. Tory nephew of Peter Legh of Lyme.

Lister, Thomas (1688–1745), of Gisburn Park, nr. Clitheroe. M.P. Clitheroe 23 Apr. 1713 until his death 15 May 1745. Tory.

Leicester
[19] Huntingdon, Theophilus Hastings, 9th Earl of (1696–1746). Tory

Stamford, Harry Grey, 4th Earl of (1715–1768). (See under Staffs.) M.P. Leicestershire 16 Feb. 1738–4 Nov. 1739. Opposition Whig.

Cave, Sir Thomas, 5th Bt. (1712–1778), of Stanford Hall, Leics. M.P. Leicestershire 1741–1747, 25 Mar. 1762–1774. Tory.

Smith, Edward (*c.* 1704–1762), of Edmondthorpe, Leics. M.P. Leicestershire 1734–15 Feb. 1762. Tory.

Wigley, James (1700–1765), of Scraptoft Hall, nr. Leicester. M.P. Leicester 27 Apr. 1737–21 June 1765. Tory.

Wrighte, George (*c.* 1706–1766), of Gayhurst, Bucks and Brooksby Hall, nr. Leicester. M.P. Leicester 1727–27 Jan. 1766. Tory.

Lincoln

[20] Bristol, John Hervey, 1st Earl of (1665–1751). (See under Suffolk.) Father of Lord Hervey, the diarist, who was then in Opposition and connected with Cobham.

Haversham, Maurice Thompson, 2nd Baron (1675–1745). M.P. Bletchingley 1695–1698, Gatton 1698–1705. Opposition Whig.

Vyner, Robert (*c.* 1685–1777), of Gautby, Lincs. M.P. Great Grimsby 1710–1713, Lincolnshire 12 Feb. 1724–1761. Opposition Whig.

Whichcot, Thomas (*c.* 1700–1776), of Harpswell, Lincs. M.P. Lincolnshire 20 Feb, 1740–1774. Independent Whig who went over to Government in Jan. 1744.

Michell, John (1710–1766), of Boston, Lincs. M.P. Boston 1741–1754, 1761–30 Nov. 1766. Tory.

Proby, John (*c.* 1698–1762), of Elton Hall, Hunts. (See pp. 29, 76.) M.P. Huntingdonshire 27 Oct. 1722–1727, Stamford 1734–1747. Tory.

Middlesex

[21] Somerset, Charles Seymour, 6th Duke of (1662–1748). (See under Surrey and Wilts.) Opposition Whig.

Burlington, Richard Boyle, 3rd Earl of (1694–1753). (See under Yorkshire.) Opposition Whig; cousin of Lord Orrery.

Newdigate, Sir Roger, 5th Bt. (1719–1806), of Arbury, Warwickshire and Harefield, Middlesex. M.P. Middlesex 5 Aug. 1742–1747. Oxford University 31 Jan. 1751–1780. Tory. Refused Association.

Smithson, Sir Hugh, 4th Bt. (1715–1786), of Stanwick, Yorks and Tottenham, Middlesex. M.P. Middlesex 15 May 1740–7 Feb. 1750. Tory.

Monmouth

[22] Somerset, Lord Charles Noel (1709–1756). (See pp. 74, 77.) M.P. Monmouthshire 17 May 1731–1734, Monmouth 1734–24 Feb. 1745. Tory.

Norfolk

[23] Norfolk, Edward Howard, 9th Duke of (1688–1777). (See p. 91 and under Notts, Sussex, Yorks.) Roman Catholic implicated in the '15. His house at Worksop, Notts was searched for arms in 1745 (Chatsworth mss., Duke of Newcastle to Duke of Devonshire, 21 Nov. 1745.)

Andover, William Howard, Visct. (1714–1756). (See p. 25.) Son of 11th Earl of Suffolk. M.P. Castle Rising 16 Apr. 1737–1747. Tory.

Jerningham, Sir George, 5th Bt. (1680–1774), of Costessey, Norfolk. Roman Catholic.

Andrews, Sir Francis, 4th Bt. (d. 1759), of Denton, Norfolk. Roman Catholic.

Wodehouse, Armine (c. 1714–1777), of Kimberley Hall, Norfolk. M.P. Norfolk 23 Mar. 1737–1768. Tory.

Northampton

[24] Isham, Edmund, 6th Bt. (1690–1772), of Lamport Hall, Northants. M.P. Northamptonshire 31 Mar. 1737–15 Dec. 1772. Tory.

Cartwright, Thomas (1671–1748), of Aynho, Northants. M.P. Northamptonshire 1695–1698, 1701–10 Mar. 1748. Tory.

Parker, Armstead (c. 1699–1777), of Burghberry Manor, Peterborough, Northants. M.P. Peterborough 29 Jan. 1734–1741, 3 May 1742–1747, 1761–1768. Tory.

Shirley, Hon. Sewallis (1709–1765). M.P. Brackley 22 Mar. 1742–1754, Callington 1754–1761. Opposition Whig returned by Duke of Bridgwater.

Wortley Montagu, Edward (1678–1761), of Wortley, Yorks. M.P. Huntingdon 1705–1713, Westminster 1715–1722, Huntingdon 1722–1734, Peterborough 1734–1761. Opposition Whig. Husband of Lady Mary Wortley Montagu.

Northumberland

[25] Derwentwater, Charles Radcliffe, but for attainder 5th Earl of (1693–1746). Taken on way from France to join rebellion in Scotland, and executed 11 Dec. 1746. Roman Catholic.

Widdrington, Henry Francis, but for attainder 5th Baron (1701–1774). Son of one of the leaders of the '15. Roman Catholic.

Swinburne, Sir John, 3rd Bt. (1698–1745), of Capheaton, Northumb. Roman Catholic.

Fenwick, John (1698–1747), of Stanton, Brinkburn and Bywell, Northumb. M.P. Northumberland 1741–19 Dec. 1747. Tory.

Blackett, Sir Walter, 2nd Bt. (1707–1777), of Wallington Hall, Northumb. M.P. Newcastle-upon-Tyne 1734–14 Feb. 1777. Tory.

Nottingham

[26] Middleton, Francis Willoughby, 2nd Baron (1692–1758). (See under Warwickshire.) M.P. Nottinghamshire 1713–1722, Tamworth 1722–1727. Wealthy Tory.

Trevor, Thomas, 2nd Baron (1692–1753). Son of Tory peer. Opposition Whig.

Levinz, William (c. 1713–1765), of Grove and Bilby, Notts. M.P. Nottinghamshire 1734–1747. Tory.

Warren, Borlase (1677–1747), of Stapleford, Notts. M.P. Nottingham 1713–1715, 1727–15 May 1747. Tory.

Oxford

[27] Lichfield, George Henry Lee, 3rd Earl of (1718–1772). (See pp. 77–8.) M.P. Oxfordshire 27 Feb. 1740–15 Feb. 1743. Tory. Lord of Bedchamber to George III.

Dashwood, Sir James, 2nd Bt. (1715–1779), of Kirtlington Park, Oxon. M.P.

Oxfordshire 30 Jan. 1740–1754, 1761–1768. Tory. Refused association in 1745.

Butler, Edward (*c.* 1686–1745), of Burleigh Park, Leics. M.P. Oxford University 31 Mar. 1737–29 Oct. 1745. Tory. Died before rebellion.

Rowney, Thomas (*c.* 1693–1759), of Dean Farm, Oxon. M.P. Oxford 1722–27 Oct. 1759. Tory.

Herbert, Philip (1716–1749), of Tythorp, Bucks. M.P. Oxford 3 Dec. 1740–1749. Tory.

Dawkins, James (*c.* 1696–1766), of Over Norton, Oxon. M.P. New Woodstock 1734–1747. Tory returned by Duchess of Marlborough.

Moore, William (1699–1746), of Polesden Lacey, Surrey. M.P. Banbury 25 Nov. 1740–26 Oct. 1746. Opposition Whig. Son of Bolingbroke's friend Arthur Moore.

Rutland

²⁸ Noel, Hon. James (1711–1752), of Exton, Rutland. M.P. Rutland 1734–17 June 1752. Tory. Son of Lord Gainsborough.

Shropshire

²⁹ Astley, Sir John, 2nd Bt. (1687–1771), of Patshull, Staffs. M.P. Shrewsbury 1727–1734, Shropshire 1734–29 Dec. 1771. Tory. Went to see Charles Edward in France in 1752 in connection with Prussian Plot.

Corbet, Sir Richard, 4th Bt. (1696–1774), of Longnor, Salop. M.P. Shrewsbury 9 Apr. 1723–1727, 1734–1754. Whig.

Kynaston, Edward (1709–1772), of Garth, Mont. and Hardwick, Salop. M.P. Bishop's Castle 1734–1741 and Montgomeryshire 1747–18 May 1772. Tory and friend of Sir Watkin Williams Wynn. Other Kynastons were presumably his kinsmen rather than William Kynaston M.P. Shrewsbury 1734–24 Feb. 1749 who was a government Whig.

Lyster, Richard (*c.* 1692–1766), of Rowton Castle, Salop. M.P. Shrewsbury 1722–9 Apr. 1723, 1727–1734, Shropshire 11 Dec. 1740–13 Aug. 1766. Tory.

Somerset

³⁰ Chapman, Sir John, 2nd Bt. (*c.* 1710–1781), of Cockenhatch, Barkway, Herts. M.P. Taunton 1741–1747. Opposition Whig.

Portman, Henry William (*c.* 1709–1761), of Orchard Portman, Somerset. M.P. Taunton 1734–1741, Somerset 1741–1747. Tory.

Prowse, Thomas (*c.* 1707–1767), of Compton Bishop, Somerset. (See p. 104.) M.P. Somerset 26 Nov. 1740–1 Jan. 1767. Moderate Tory.

Buck, John (1703–1745), of Bideford, Devon. M.P. Taunton 1741 until his death 3 April 1745.

Carew, Thomas (1702–1766), of Crowcombe, nr. Minehead, Somerset. (See pp. 32, 85.) M.P. Minehead 9 Feb. 1739–1747. Tory. Opposed subscriptions.

Dodington, George Bubb (*c.* 1691–1762), of Eastbury, Dorset. (See pp. 26–7.) M.P. Winchelsea 1715–1722, Bridgwater 1722–1754, Weymouth and Melcombe Regis 1754–1761. Leading Opposition Whig.

Harvey, Michael (1694–1748), of Coombe, Surrey and Clifton Maybank, nr.

Milborne Port, Somerset. M.P. Milborne Port 10 June–6 July 1717, 1722–1741, 2 Feb. 1742–1747. Tory.

Southampton

[31] Shaftesbury, Anthony Ashley Cooper, 4th Earl of (1711–1771). Opposition Whig. Son-in-law of Lord Gainsborough; his wife was a Roman Catholic convert (Aveling, 260).

Barrington, Sir John, 7th Bt. (d. 1776), of Swainstown, I. of W. M.P. Newtown I. of W. 25 Apr. 1729–1734, 1741–Nov. 1775. Opposition Whig.

Delmé, Peter (1710–1770), of Quarley, nr. Andover, Hants. M.P. Ludgershall 1734–1741, Southampton 1741–1754. Opposition Whig.

Gibbon, Edward (1707–1770), of Putney, Surrey. (See p. 40.) M.P. Petersfield 1734–1741, Southampton 1741–1747. Tory.

Stafford

[32] Shrewsbury, George Talbot, 14th Earl of (1719–1787). (See under Worcestershire and Yorkshire.) Roman Catholic.

Berkshire, Henry Howard, 5th Earl of (1687–1757). (See under Wilts.) Tory. Succeeded his cousin as 11th Earl of Suffolk 22 Apr. 1745. During the '45 received a protection from Charles Edward dated Kendal 24 Nov. 1745 (*HMC 10th Rep.* iv 346).

Audley, James Touchet, 17th Lord (1723–1769). Roman Catholic.

Stourton, Charles, 11th Baron (1702–1753). R. C. A poor lord (Aveling 262).

Gower, John Leveson, 1st Baron (1694–1754). (See pp. 44, 99 and under Yorks.).

Ward, John, 6th Baron (1704–1774), of Sedgley Park, Staffs. M.P. Newcastle-under-Lyme 1727–1734. Tory.

Leigh, Thomas, 4th Baron (1713–1749). Tory.

Chetwynd, John, 2nd Visct. [1] (1680–1767), of Ingestre Hall, Staffs. M.P. St. Mawes 1715–1722, Stockbridge 1722–1734, Stafford 31 Jan. 1738–1747. Opposition Whig. Friend of Bolingbroke (Add. 35558ff. 3, 7); associated with Lord Gower in Staffordshire.

Bagot, Sir Walter Wagstaffe, 5th Bt. (1702–1768), of Blithfield, Staffs. (See p. 107). M.P. Newcastle-under-Lyme 20 Nov. 1724–1727, Staffordshire 1727–1734, Oxford University 16 Dec. 1762–20 Jan. 1768. Tory.

Holte, Sir Lister, 5th Bt. (1720–1770), of Aston, Warwks. (See p. 107.) M.P. Lichfield 1741–1747. Tory.

Fowler, Sir William, 3rd Bt. (*c.* 1716–1746), of Harnage Grange, Salop. Tory.

Wolseley, Sir William, 5th Bt. (1697–1769), of Wolseley, Staffs. (Howard, *Vis. England and Wales*, Notes xiv 31). Probably Tory.

Ridgley, Sir William, prob. a member of Ridgley or Rugeley family of Stafford.

Leveson-Gower, Messrs. (See p. 76.) Hon. William (*c.* 1696–1756). M.P. Staffordshire 29 Dec. 1720–13 Dec. 1756. Tory, and Hon. Baptist (*c.* 1703–1782). M.P. Newcastle-under-Lyme 1727–1761. Tory. Lord Gower's brothers.

Venables Vernon, George (1710–1780), of Sudbury, Derbyshire and Kinderton, Cheshire. See p. 76. M.P. Lichfield 20 May 1731–1747, Derby 1754–Apr. 1762. Tory.

Wilbraham, Randle (*c.* 1695–1770), of Rode Hall, nr. Congleton, Cheshire. (See pp. 76, 105.) M.P. Newcastle-under-Lyme 26 Nov. 1740–1747. Appleby 1747–1754, Newton 1754–1768. Tory.

Lane, Col. John (1669–1748), of King's Bromley, Staffs. Grandson of Col. John Lane who saved Charles II after the battle of Worcester (Burke, *Commoners* i 174). Tory.

Suffolk

[33] Firebrace, Sir Cordell, 3rd Bt. (1712–1759), of Long Melford, Suffolk. M.P. Suffolk 5 Mar. 1735–28 Mar. 1759. Tory.

Affleck, John (1710–1776), of Dalham Hall, Suffolk. M.P. Suffolk 23 Mar. 1743–1761, Amersham 4 Dec. 1767–1768. Tory.

Hanmer, Sir Thomas, 4th Bt. (1677–1746), of Mildenhall, Suffolk. M.P. Thetford 19 Mar. 1701–1702, Flintshire 1702–1705, Thetford 1705–1708, Suffolk 1708–1727. Former Hanoverian Tory, who retired from political life after the accession of George II.

Surrey

[34] Butler, Charles, 1st Baron Butler of Weston (1671–1758). Better known as Earl of Arran [1]. (See pp. 12, 110.) Tory.

St. John, John, 11th Baron St. John de Bletso (d. 1757). Tory.

Mountjoy, Herbert Windsor, 2nd Baron (1707–1758). M.P. Cardiff Boroughs 1734–8 June 1738. Tory.

Thrale, Ralph (*c.* 1698–1758), of Streatham, Surrey. M.P. Southwark 1741–1747. Opposition Whig. Father-in-law of Dr Johnson's friend Mrs Thrale.

Newland, George (*c.* 1692–1749), of Gatton, Surrey. M.P. Gatton 16 May 1738–22 Oct. 1749. Tory.

Hervey, John (1696–1746), of East Betchworth, Reigate, Surrey. M.P. Reigate 16 Feb. 1739–1741, Wallingford 1754–30 July 1764. Whig.

Scawen, Thomas (d. 1774), of Carshalton, Surrey. M.P. Surrey 12 Apr. 1727–1741. Opposition Whig.

Woodroffe, George (d. 1779), of Albury and Farnham, Surrey. Stood unsuccessfully for Surrey in March 1742 (Manning and Bray, *Surrey* iii 175–6). Tory.

Sussex

[35] Montacute, Anthony Browne, 6th Visct. Montacute or Montagu (1686–1767). Roman Catholic.

Caryll, John Baptist (1716–1788), of Ladyholt, Surrey. (See pp. 43, 55–6.) Roman Catholic.

Goring, Sir Charles, 5th Bt. (1706–1769), of Highden, and Wiston, Sussex. His father was one of the leaders of the Atterbury Plot, and his younger brother Henry became a member of Charles Edward's household in 1746. Tory.

Fagg, Sir William, 5th Bt. (d. 1791) of Mystole, nr. Canterbury, Kent. A relation of the Gorings.

Peachey, Sir John, 2nd Bt. (*c.* 1680–1744), of West Dean, Sussex. M.P. Midhurst 3 Feb. 1738–9 April 1744. Opposition Whig.

Campion, Henry (d. 1761), of Danny Place, in Hurstpierpoint, Sussex. M.P. East Grinstead 1708–1710, Sussex 1713–1715. Active Jacobite in 1715 (see *HMC Stuart* i and vi).

Kemp, Anthony (c. 1663–1753), of Slindon, Sussex. Probably Tory.

Webster, Whisler (d. 1779), of Battle Abbey, Sussex. M.P. East Grinstead 1741–1761. Opposition Whig.

Caryll, Richard, second son of Pope's friend John Caryll. Became a Jesuit (see H. Erskine-Hill 62, 93).

Warwick
36 Denbigh, William Feilding, 5th Earl of (1697–1755). Tory. Lived in France 'in the middle of a fine vineyard three miles from Lyons'.

Northampton, James Compton, 5th Earl of (1687–1754). M.P. Warwickshire 1710–1711. Tory.

Hereford, Price Devereux, 10th Visct. (1694–1748). M.P. Montgomeryshire 9 Jan. 1719–3 Oct. 1740. Tory. Friend of Sir Watkin Williams Wynn.

Brooke, Francis Greville, 8th Baron Brooke (1719–1773). Tory.

Throgmorton, Sir Robert, 4th Bt. (1702–1791), of Coughton Court, Warwks. Roman Catholic.

Mordaunt, Sir Charles, 6th Bt. (c. 1697–1778), of Walton D'Eiville, nr. Kineton, Warwks. M.P. Warwickshire 6 Feb. 1734–1774. Wealthy Tory.

Digby, Hon. Edward (c. 1693–1746), of Wandsworth, Surrey. M.P. Warwickshire 11 May 1726–2 Oct. 1746. Moderate Tory.

Sheldon, William (1715–1779), of Beoley, Worcs and Studley, Warwks. Roman Catholic (Nash, *Worcs* i 54).

Carrington, probably Francis, owner of the manor of Drayton in Stratford-on-Avon (*VCH, Warwks* iii 266n.).

Berkley, probably Thomas, of Spetchley, Worcs who was related to the Darells of Kent (Nash, *Worcs* ii 358; Burke, *Commoners* i 471).

Grove, William (1702–1767), of Honiley, Warwks. M.P. Coventry 1741–1761. Tory.

Farmer, John (c. 1700–1764), lord of the manor of Oldbury (VCH, *Warwks* iv 122).

Perkins, John (1711–1744), of Orton-on-the-Hill, Leics and Witherley, Warwks. Related to Sir William Perkins executed as a Jacobite in 1696 (Nichols, *Leics* iv 454).

Westmorland
37 Musgrave, Sir Philip, 6th Bt. (c. 1712–1795), of Edenhall, Cumberland. M.P. Westmorland 1741–1747. Tory.

Wilts
38 St. John, John, 2nd Visct. (1702–1748). M.P. Wootton Bassett 1727–1734. Tory. Half-brother of Bolingbroke. His mother was French and he was educated in France.

Bouverie, Sir Jacob, 3rd Bt. (c. 1694–1761), of Longford Castle, Wilts. M.P. Salisbury 1741–1747. Tory.

Seymour, Sir Edward, 6th Bt. (1695–1757), of Maiden Bradley, Wilts. M.P. Salisbury 1741–1747. Tory.

Turner, Sir Edward, 2nd Bt. (1719–1766), of Ambrosden, Oxon. M.P. Great Bedwyn 1741–1747, Oxfordshire 23 Apr. 1755–1761, Penryn 1761–21 Oct. 1766. Tory.

Popham, Edward (*c.* 1711–1772), of Littlecote, Wilts. M.P. Great Bedwyn 5 Apr. 1738–1741, Wiltshire 1741–14 July 1772. Tory.

Grenville, James (1715–1783). M.P. Old Sarum 5 Jan. 1742–May 1747, Bridport 1747–1754, Buckingham 1754–1768, Horsham 1768–Mar. 1770. Opposition Whig, one of the Cobham cubs.

Pitt, William (1708–1778), of Hayes, Kent. (See p. 90.) M.P. Old Sarum 18 Feb. 1735–1747, Seaford 1747–1754, Aldborough 1754–Dec. 1756, Buckingham 7–11 Dec. 1756, Okehampton 11 Dec. 1756–July 1757, Bath 9 July 1757–4 Aug. 1766. Opposition Whig and a Cobham cub. Later 1st Earl of Chatham.

Thursby, John Harvey (*c.* 1711–1764), of Abingdon Abbey, Northants. M.P. Wootton Bassett 1741–1747, Stamford 1754–1761. Tory.

Neale, Robert (1706–1776), of Corsham, Wilts. M.P. Wootton Bassett 1741–1754. Whig and Government supporter. Badly in debt.

Crawley, John (1703–1767), of Stockwood Park, Beds. M.P. Marlborough 28 Feb. 1737–1747. Tory.

Worcester

[39] Coventry, William, 5th Earl of (*c.* 1676–1751). M.P. Bridport 1708–27 Oct. 1719. Opposition Whig.

Lechmere, Edmund (1710–1805), of Hanley Castle, Worcs. M.P. Worcestershire 1734–1747. Tory.

Pytts, Edmund (*c.* 1696–1753), of Kyre, nr. Tenbury, Worcs. M.P. Worcestershire 1741–24 Nov. 1753. Tory.

Foley, Thomas (1716–1777), of Stoke Edith Court, Herefs. M.P. Droitwich 1741–1747, 9–16 Dec. 1747, 1754–1768, Herefordshire 1768–10 May 1776. Tory.

York

[40] Carlisle, Henry Howard, 4th Earl of (1693–1758). (p. 32) M.P. Morpeth 1715–1738. Opposition Whig.

Langdale, Marmaduke, 4th Lord (d. 1771). Roman Catholic.

Stapylton, Sir Miles, 4th Bt. (*c.* 1708–1752), of Myton, Yorks. M.P. Yorkshire 1734–Apr. 1750. Tory. Took subscriptions in 1745 (Chatsworth mss., Will Hewett to Duke of Devonshire, 27 Sept. 1745).

Slingsby, Sir Henry, 5th Bt. (*c.* 1693–1763), of Scriven, nr. Knaresborough. (See pp. 43, 47.) M.P. Knaresborough 17 May 1714–1715, 1722–18 Jan. 1763. Tory.

Fox, George (*c.* 1696–1773), of Bramham Park, Yorks. M.P. Hindon 1734–1741, York 21 July 1742–1761. Tory. Took subscriptions in 1745 (Chatsworth mss., Will Hewett to Duke of Devonshire, 27 Sept. 1745).

Aislabie, William (*c.* 1699–1781), of Studley Royal, nr. Ripon, Yorks. M.P. Ripon 1 Apr. 1721–17 May 1781. Opposition Whig, who went over to Government in 1744.

Berkeley, Hon. George (*c.* 1692–1746), of Marble Hill, Twickenham, Mdx. M.P. Dover 20 Dec. 1720–1734, Hedon 1734–1741, 4 Mar. 1742–29 Oct. 1746. Opposition Whig.

Pelham, Charles (*c.* 1679–1763), of Brocklesby, Lincs. M.P. Great Grimsby 1722–1727, Beverley 2 Feb. 1738–1754. Tory.

Wales

[41] Powis, William Herbert, 2nd Marquess of (*c.* 1665–1745). Duke of Powis in Jacobite peerage. Arrested as a Jacobite suspect 1696, 1715 and 1722. Roman Catholic who conformed. Died 22 Oct. 1745.

Bulkeley, James, 6th Visct. [1] (1717–1752), of Baron Hill, Anglesey. M.P. Beaumaris 20 April 1739–23 April 1752. Tory and friend of Sir Watkin Williams Wynn.

Wynn, Sir Watkin Williams, 3rd Bt. (*c.* 1693–1749), of Wynnstay, Denbighshire. (See pp. 41–2.) M.P. Denbighshire 30 June 1716–1741, Montgomeryshire 1741–23 Feb. 1742, Denbighshire 23 Feb. 1742–20 Sept. 1749. Tory.

City of London and Westminster

[42] At the Westminster election of May 1741, when the Government saw that its candidates were about to be defeated, troops were called in to close the poll. In one of the crucial divisions before the fall of Walpole the Westminster election was declared void. At the ensuing by-election on 31 December 1741 the Independent Electors of Westminster secured the return of Edward Vernon, an Opposition Whig and a popular hero (see pp. 98–9), and of Charles Edwin, a Tory (*HC* i 285–6).

Appendix II

List of the Corporation of London
given to Butler 1743

After private talks with Robert Willimot, Robert Westley, George Heathcote, Edward Gibbon, William Benn and Daniel Lambert (see pp. 40–1), Butler was given the following list of the corporation of London and an account of its constitution (AEM & D. Ang. 85f. 106) Balhaldy took a copy with some minor variants which he sent to the Pretender (Stuart mss. 254/154). Those marked with an asterisk took the subscriptions and or the Association (see p. 84–5) in September–October 1745 (from information kindly supplied by Dr. Nicholas Rogers).

J = Jacobite
P = Patriot
H = Hanoverian
W = Whig

A list of the names of the lord mayor, aldermen, recorder and sheriffs of the City of London together with the deputies and common councilmen of the several wards for the year 1743 as they are returned by the ward mote inquests in their respective indentures.

The Rt. Honourable Robert Willimot Esq. Lord Mayor J.P.*	Lime Street
Sir John Eyles Bart. H.W. Seldom or scarce ever attends. Post Master General	Bridge Without
Sir Robert Baylis Knt. H.W. Attends. Commissioner of the customs*	Bread Street
Sir William Billers Knt. H.W. Generally attends. Director of the East India Company	Cordwainer
Sir Edward Bellamy W. Seldom attends, old and very infirm*	Billingsgate

Sir John Thompson Knt. H.W. Seldom attends because infirm*	Candlewick
Sir John Barnard Knt. Turned H. Seldom attends*	Dowgate
Micajah Perry Esq., H.W. Dying of a dropsy. Not able ever to attend	Aldgate
Sir John Salter Knt. H.W. Director of the East India Company	Cornhill
Daniel Lambert Esq. J.P.*	Tower
George Heathcote Esq. P. Against the Court	Walbrook
Sir Harcourt Master Knt. H.W. Court pensioner	Coleman Street
Sir George Champion Knt. Renegado. Bribed for which famous*	Bridge Within
Sir Joseph Hankey Knt. W.*	Langhorn
Robert Westley Esq., J.P. Next the chair	Queenhithe
Henry Marshal Esq. J.P.*	Farringdon Within
William Baker Esq., W. Director of the East India Company*	Bassisshaw
George Arnold Esq. W.*	Cheap
Richard Hoare Esq., J.P.*	Farringdon Without
William Benn Esq. J.P.*	Aldersgate
Robert Ladbrooke Esq. J.P.*	Castle Baynard
William Calvert Esq. J.P.	Portsoken
Walter Barnard Esq. J.P.	Broad Street
Samuel Pennant Esq. P. Against the Court	Bishopsgate
Edward Gibbon Esq. J.P.	Vintry
John Blachford J.P.*	Cripplegate Within and Without

Simon Urlin, Serjeant-at-law. Recorder W.
  Against the Court (indifferent)
William Benn Esq. J.P. sheriff
Charles Eggleton sheriff, of no consequence
John Bosworth Esq. chamberlain J.P.
Thomas Garrard Esq., common serjeant,
  indifferent
Miles Man Esq., town clerk J.P.

The names of the deputies and common councilmen of the several
  wards

Aldersgate 8
Major John Snart deputy J.P.
Joseph Rose J.P.

Richard Bayley J.P.
John Underwood J.P.
Samuel Ballard deputy J.P.*

Robert Henshaw J.P.
Richard Reily J.P.*
Nathaniel Maccascree J.P.

Aldgate 6
Thomas Stanford deputy P.
Christopher Fullagar J.P.*
Thomas Harrison H.W.*
John Hall J.P.
Thomas Sharp J.P.
William Pond J.P.

Bassishaw 4
William Coulhurst deputy H.W.*
Francis Cooper H.W.*
Samuel Fludyer H.W.*
Samuel Ellis H.W.*

Billingsgate 10
Edmund Stevens deputy P.
William Parker J.P.
Samuel Harris H.W.
Edward Robinson J.P.
Henry Cowling H.W.
Robert Peck H.W.
Thomas Crozier H.W.
Robert Rossiter H.
George Woods J.P.
Thomas Winterbottom H.

Bishopsgate 14
James Dunsie deputy J.P.
George Wylde J.P.*
Daniel Davies J.P.
Thomas Long J.P.
Samuel Vickers J.P.
William Munday J.P.
William Poole J.P.
Francis Cockayne J.P.
Peter Roberts J.P.
Robert Fawdery J.P.
John Holland deputy J.P.*
Henry Wily J.P.

John Forty J.P.*
William Hookham J.P.

Breadstreet 12
Robert Cady deputy H.W.*
John Sedgwick H.W.*
William Wooley H.W.*
Anthony Plank H.W.
John Todd H.W.*
Richard Witts H.W.*
James Budgette H.W.*
Thomas Morris H.W.*
Thomas Smith H.W.*
Heneage Robinson J.P.*
Anthony Lucas J.P.
John Ogilvie H.W.

Bridge 15
Richard Clay deputy J.P.*
Cornelius Herbert J.P.
Thomas Durnford J.P.*
James Hodges J.P.*
Michael Methens J.P.
Benjamin Tyson J.P.
Ambrose Hammond J.P.*
William White J.P.
John Cooper J.P.
Christopher Taylor J.P.*
Stephen Cooper J.P.
James Heywood J.P.*
Joseph Gonson J.P.*
George Baskerville J.P.*
Thomas Pritchard J.P.

Broadstreet 10
John Clarke deputy J.P.*
Ralph Wilson J.P.
Thomas Eden J.P.
Hugh Knowlings J.P.
John Low J.P.
Timothy Helmsley J.P.*
Robert Bishop Esq. J.P.
John Mitford J.P.

Broadstreet 10—cont.
William Whitaker J.P.*
William Chapman J.P.

Candlewick 8
Samuel Osborne deputy H.W.*
William Arnold H.W.
Peter Thomas Esq. H.W.
Edward Yeates H.W.
John Blacksley H.W.
Thomas Mallett H.W.*
George Hoare H.W.*
Arthur Lane H.W.

Castlebaynard 10
William Hunt deputy J.P.
Benjamin Crook J.P.*
Nathaniel Nash J.P.*
John Willis J.P.
Robert Territt J.P.
Thomas Powell J.P.
John Winder J.P.*
William Giles J.P.*
William Lord J.P.
John Cordwell J.P.*

Cheap 12
Thomas Wright deputy W.
Samuel Sedgwick wavers*
Robert Waite J.P.
Edward Southhouse J.P.
George Verney J.P.
Waller Hayter J.P.
Theodore Cock H.W.
Leonard Read H.W.*
Frederick Stanton H.W.
Windmill Compton wavers
John Skinner wavers
Thomas Smith H.W.*

Coleman Street 6
Thomas Wilkinson deputy H.W.
Edward Roberts H.W.

Robert Lovick Esq. H.W.
John Lloyd H.W.*
Thomas Gibson Esq. H.W.
Wm. Hayter H.W.*

Cordwainer 8
John Daye deputy J.P.*
George Smith J.P.
Percival Pott J.P.*
Francis Grissel J.P.*
Josiah Colebrooke J.P.*
Henry Spencer J.P.*
William Reynolds J.P.*
Richard Blunt J.P.*

Cornhill 6
George Townsend J.P.
William Meadows J.P.
John Young J.P.*
James Walton J.P.*
Francis Ellis J.P.
Bourchier Cleeve J.P.

Cripplegate Within 8
Thomas Elton deputy J.P.*
Richard Molineux J.P.
Thomas Nichol J.P.
William Sims J.P.
Robert Elliot J.P.
Thomas Scott J.P.
Charles Hartley J.P.
James Mount J.P.*

Cripplegate Without 4
Richard Farington deputy J.P.
William Cooper J.P.
John Wallington J.P.
Thomas Bourne J.P.

Dowgate 8
Thomas Curryer deputy J.P.*
Peter Hambley J.P.*

William Ford J.P.
Richard Swithin J.P.*
Thomas Rhodes J.P.
William Stephenson J.P.*
Samuel Stretton J.P.
Christopher Robinson J.P.*

Faringdon Within 17
Richard Sclater deputy J.P.*
Richard Skinner J.P.
Robert Stringer J.P.*
James Price J.P.
Michael Martindale J.P.*
Jenner Swaine J.P.
Thomas Hodges J.P.*
John Humphreys J.P.
Giles Mills J.P.
Thomas Fawson J.P.
Henry Sisson J.P.
Richard Holland J.P.
John Reeve J.P.
Samuel Scawell J.P.*
John Blackhall J.P.
Robert Willes J.P.
Richard Grainger J.P.

Faringdon Without 16
St. Sepulchres
Robert Gammon J.P.*
Cadwallader Coker J.P.*
Charles Taylor Ballard J.P.
Edward Walmesley J.P.
John King J.P.*
Christopher Myngs J.P.*

St. Andrew Holborn
Thomas Nash deputy J.P.
Christopher Horsenail J.P.*

St. Dunstan West
John Child deputy J.P.
William Hart J.P.
Samuel Cranmer J.P.*

St. Brides
Philip Robinson J.P.
Samuel Rutter J.P.*
George Grainger J.P.*

St. Martin's Ludgate
Richard Nutt J.P.
George Burton J.P.

Langborn 10
Thomas Oyles deputy dead
William Pepys H.W.
Edward Neale H.W.
Thomas Minors H.W.
Henry Lawton H.W.
Robert Wilson J.P.*
Edward Ironside J.P.
John Barker J.P.
John Townsend J.P.
Thomas Rawlinson H.W.

Limestreet 4
Giles Vincent deputy J.P.*
Samuel Southouse J.P.*
John Fleetwood J.P.
George Mason J.P.

Portsoken 5
Robert Pyecroft deputy J.P.
John McKellan J.P.*
Richard Bridgman J.P.
William Myers J.P.
Crispe Gascoyne Esq. J.P.

Queenhithe 6
Joseph Ayliffe deputy J.P.
Robert Allsop J.P.
George Nelson J.P.
Edward Davis J.P.
Charles Bland J.P.
Thomas Northey J.P.

Tower 12
Samuel Tatem deputy J.P.*

Tower 12—cont.
William Cleaver J.P.
James Phillips J.P.
William Prowting J.P.*
John Sellar J.P.
Thomas Green J.P.
Robert Booth Esq. J.P.
John Woodbridge J.P.
Jonathan Granger J.P.
Daniel Lambert J.P.*
Henry Seale J.P.
Richard Romman J.P.*

Vintry 9
Thomas Gregg deputy H.W.*
James Kelham J.P.
William Beddel H.W.*

William Mills H.W.*
Thomas Parker H.W.
Martin Wardell H.W.*
William Hoggard H.W.
Marsh Dickenson H.W.
Thomas Rous Esq. H.W.[1]

Walbrook 8
William Wilkins deputy H.W.
Robert Peirce Esq, J.P.
Col. Richard Martin J.P.
William Farmer J.P.
James Ennis J.P.*
Francis Flower Esq. J.P.
Basil Brown J.P.*
William Arnold J.P.

Total 236

The city of London is governed by twenty six aldermen one of which is lord mayor and presides universally in the City, the serjeant-at-law, two hundred and thirty six common councilmen, twenty six whereof are deputies of the aldermen, a recorder, two sheriffs, a chamberlain, a city common serjeant, and town clerk.

This number of twenty six aldermen arises from the division of the city in twenty six districts or divisions, by the citizens called wards. Each ward chooses its own aldermen, whose office is for life and such a regular number of common councilmen as they have a right to, who may be all changed or continued every Michaelmas by the ward, save the alderman's deputy of the ward named by the alderman and ward.

When this body meets, which is as often as the lord mayor pleases besides their regular day of meeting, the court is named the lord mayor, aldermen and common council of the city, and they have many principal powers, privileges and immunities for the government of the City in general, powers in whatever regards the policy of the city or conduct of the citizens, save so far as particular corporations have charters given from the Crown, with special privileges for the policy of their corporation; in their court of assistants, as they name them, the members of these corporations are odd of eighty; each of which have their chart of assistance with different privileges and exemptions as favoured by the King granted of these charters.

I have observed that each ward has the sole right of choosing its own

---

[1] Will be changed as Gibbon is alderman.

alderman; this is done in a court held by the lord mayor for that effect within the ward wherein each freeman of the ward has a voice, by which it happens that the inclinations and temper of the ward is known by the choice of their alderman, but much better by the choice they make of their common councilmen, because the alderman for the ward, once chosen, is for life, and often for fifty years past, has dissembled till once named, that he came out of their power; whereas the common councilmen are once a year at their mercy.

Tho every freeman in each ward have the power or privilege of choosing their own alderman, yet the whole freemen of the City have not a voice in naming the mayor, nor any of them unless he be entered and of a particular corporation or company; the body of freemen entered in this manner are named the livery of the city; twelve companies whereof are designed the greater companies and the number of the whole is computed betwixt eight and nine thousand. This livery has the right of presenting two each year qualified for being lord mayor; one of which the body of aldermen must name mayor. In this the livery seldom offer any other for mayor, but the senior alderman, commonly designed next in the chair, and who is highly affronted when disappointed as being marked out by the City as infamous, which seldom happens save in such extraordinary cases as Champion's.[1] The livery has likeways the power of naming their sheriffs, with this they often divert themselves at the expense of the rich men they judge will not officiate, they having it in their choice to accept or pay what they name a fine to some hundred pounds sterling, but in this sometimes they are bit, the person named accepting contrary to what they judged and that they become burdened with a sheriff to vex them. It has the privilege also of choosing the City's representatives in Parliament from this flows the first figure the City has made by its representatives in Parliament.

Notwithstanding the presumption of learning the certain temper of the citizens by the choice of their aldermen, yet this has been for a long time a very uncertain mark, because the administration uses, with all the power, interest and even money of the Crown and by all manner of art to divert and corrupt the natural bent of the people. When it happened that the body of the city or ward was on their guard, as it sometimes was, it disappointed all their art, power and influence, by the force of a very great majority, they always showed at least for twenty eight years past, when heedful, to make that majority exert itself. But even then, the City or ward was often frustrated by the alderman it had forced on the administration by his changing sides. It was not so easy a matter to corrupt the common councilmen, because the purchase would have been very

[1] George Champion, passed over as lord mayor for voting against the Spanish Convention in 1739 (*HC* i 541).

expensive, so often repeated; the corruption could last but one year; the corrupted then returned under the power and consequently the disgrace of their fellow citizens, and for this reason the majority of common councilmen has for twenty-eight years past been of the side of nature, justice and the true interest of the community.

This will make it appear a paradox, how it came about that for some time every question was carried on against the opinion of the majority of the city court. But the paradox ceases when it is informed that the majority of the aldermen have a negative in any question where the common councilmen, and they divide,[1] which tho the majority of aldermen seldom made use of because extremely disagreeable to the body of the city, yet they sometimes have made use of it and have it always in their power, for this reason the majority of common councilmen became careless of attendance, while there was a great majority of aldermen against them which gave an opportunity to the other party, to carry whatever they had in mind, and made the majority of common councilmen very careful not to push anything against the bent of their aldermen, who by this negative and other powers inherent in the body of aldermen over the city and in each particular alderman over his ward, have great weight and influence in bringing about what they have a mind to; by this it happens that the body of aldermen were enabled to supply the place of any of their number that died which are of a kidney with themselves and administration, or the administration purchased him when chosen against its interest. But the City in the case of their renegade Champion has noted that desertion with such marks of infamy and disgrace, that hardly any other will ever dare to follow his example. It flows from this spirit of honour, virtue and resentment, that the city now makes such a leading figure in the kingdom, and has got so far the better of a poisoned body of aldermen supported and assisted by all the power, authority and money of the Crown, as to have supplied the room of any that deceased with one of the same genius within the City till they have got a majority of aldermen of their side, and that the Administration has given over making any opposition to it, or meddling in the City's affairs because the Administration find that opposition only serves to augment the zeal and application of the City.

It will then appear a question not very difficult to answer, how a body of people living in a society governed by a lord mayor and a majority of aldermen, against thirteen aldermen some of what are indifferent which side prevail, and the greatest part so superannuat and infirm, as not to be able to attend, and this majority of aldermen joined and supported by a

[1] For the circumstances of the Act of Parliament imposing the aldermen's veto over the decisions of the court of common council, see *HC* i 280.

hundred and fifty three common council men J.P. of the same mind and disposition with the people and about thirty more Patriot for the people against fifty H.W. some of which waver and will be changed as their aldermen die, who in the mean time seldom attend, because when present in their courts serve only for cyphers, especially when those such as Calvert, Benn, deputy Dunzie and others, I demand how will they do when it is put in their power to act naturally and according to their inclinations.

But if even yet it should be doubted that doubt cannot remain when informed that the City have chosen the most zealous and distinguished Patriots governors of their public hospitals, and its advisers in affairs of moment with Sir John Hynde Cotton, Sir Watkin Williams Wynn, the Earl of Lichfield, Sir William Carew, Sir John St. Aubyn, Sir Robert Abdy, Mr. Bramston and others of the same kidney.

Chronology

1739
January   Spanish Convention
October   Declaration of war between England and Spain

1740
March   Jacobite emissary sent to England to sound Tories on prospects of a restoration

1741
13 Feb.   Motion for removal of Sir Robert Walpole defeated
April   General election, 286 Government Whigs, 136 Tories and 131 Opposition Whigs returned
August   Lord Chesterfield goes to see Duke of Ormonde at Avignon
16/27 Sept.   Pretender's letter instructing the Tories to bring down Walpole
December   Meeting of 1741 Parliament

1742
11 Feb.   Resignation of Walpole, formation of Carteret administration
12 Feb.   Meeting of Opposition at Fountain Tavern in the Strand
18 Feb.   Duke of Argyll takes the Tories to Court
10 March   Resignation of Argyll
10 Dec.   Division on taking Hanoverian troops into English pay

1743
16 June   Battle of Dettingen, George II defeats French
Aug.–Oct.   French emissary sounds Tories on prospects of a restoration

November   Preparations for French expedition to restore Stuarts begin

1744

10 Jan.   Division on continuing Hanoverian troops in English pay
14 Feb.   English Government learns secret of invasion from a French secret agent
15 Feb.   King's message to Parliament on French invasion
22 Feb./5 March   French embarkation begins at Dunkirk
24 Feb.   French fleet off Dungeness
24–26 Feb.   Storms damage English and French fleets
28 Feb./11 March   French expedition abandoned
20/31 March   France declares war on England
December   Fall of Carteret, formation of Pelham ministry in so-called Broadbottom Administration

1745

May   Battle of Fontenoy, Maurice of Saxony defeats Duke of Cumberland
23 July   Charles Edward lands in Scotland
16 Sept.   Jacobite army enters Edinburgh
21 Sept.   Defeat of Sir John Cope at Prestonpans
October   Parliament meets at Westminster
8 Nov.   Charles Edward crosses into England
17 Nov.   Carlisle surrenders
26 Nov.   Jacobite army takes Preston
29 Nov.   Charles Edward enters Manchester
4 Dec.   Jacobite army in Derby
6 Dec.   Black Friday in London
6 Dec.   Retreat from Derby
14/25 Dec.   Date set for French landing to join Charles Edward near London
19 Dec.   King's message to Parliament on threatened French invasion, Hessian troops sent for
20 Dec.   Jacobite army crosses back into Scotland

1746

17 Jan.   Defeat of General Hawley at Falkirk
11 April   Division on continuing Hanoverian troops into English pay

16 April   Battle of Culloden, Cumberland defeats Jacobite army

August   Trial of rebel Lords

29 Sept./10 Oct.   Charles Edward back in France

October   Maurice of Saxony defeats General Ligonier at Roucoux

1747

January   Trial of Lord Lovat

June–July   General election, 338 Government Whigs, 117 Tories, 97 opposition Whigs returned

July   Maurice of Saxony defeats Cumberland at Laffeldt

1748

18 Oct.   Treaty of Aix-la-Chapelle, peace made between England and France

Bibliography

1. GUIDE TO MANUSCRIPT SOURCES USED

ENGLAND

ROYAL ARCHIVES, WINDSOR CASTLE
Stuart mss.

BRITISH LIBRARY
Additional mss.
   9129–9224 William Coxe's transcripts
  32712–32805 Newcastle papers
  35337–35602 Hardwicke papers
  47098B   Egmont papers

PUBLIC RECORD OFFICE
State Papers
Series 36 Domestic, George II
Series 44 Domestic, entry books
Series 78 Foreign (France)

Granville Mss 30/29/1

OTHER COLLECTIONS
Ryder diary transcript made available to the History of Parliament Trust
by the Earl of Harrowby and the Treasurer and Masters of the Bench of
Lincoln's Inn, transcribed from the original shorthand by Mr K. L.
Perrin.
Blenheim Mss. Sunderland papers
Badminton Mss. Beaufort papers
Chatsworth Mss. Devonshire papers
Alnwick Mss. Northumberland papers
Bank of England. Morice papers
Lichfield Mss. Anson papers (transcripts in possession of the History of
    Parliament Trust)
Borlase Mss. Letters from Sir John St. Aubyn to William Borlase in
    Morrab Library by courtesy of A. Pool of Pool, Purchas & Le Grice,
    Solicitors, Penzance

11

Digby Mss. formerly in possession of Miss Fiona Digby, transcripts communicated by Howard Erskine-Hill

FRANCE

Paris

QUAI D'ORSAY (Archives du Ministère des Affaires étrangères)
Correspondance Politique, Angleterre
Mémoires et Documents, Angleterre
Correspondance Politique, Bavière

CHATEAU DE VINCENNES (Archives du Ministère de la Défense Nationale)
Guerre série AI

ARCHIVES NATIONALES (Archives du Ministère de la Marine)
Marine séries B2 and B3

Rouen

BIBLIOTHEQUE DE ROUEN
Collection Leber Richelieu papers

2. PRINTED WORKS CITED

Argenson, Marquis d', *Journal et Mémoires*, ed. E. J. B. Rathéry, 9 vols, Paris 1859–67.

Aveling, J. C., *The Handle and the Axe*, 1976.

Balteau, J., *Dictionnaire de Biographie française*, Paris 1933–76.

Barbier, E. J. F., *Journal Historique et anecdotique du règne de Louis XV*, ed. A. de Villegille, 4 vols, Paris 1847–56.

Beaven, A. B., *The Aldermen of London*, 2 vols, 1908–13.

Bennett, G. V., *The Tory Crisis in Church and State 1688–1730, The career of Francis Atterbury, Bishop of Rochester*, Oxford 1975.

Bodleian Quarterly Record, anon., 'The opening of the Radcliffe Library in 1749' i (1915), pp. 165–72.

Bongie, Laurence, 'Voltaire's English, high treason and a manifesto for Bonnie Prince Charles', *Studies on Voltaire and the eighteenth century* clxxi (1977), pp. 7–29.

Boswell, James, *Life of Johnson*, ed. G. B. Hill, rev. L. F. Powell. 6 vols, Oxford 1934–50.

Boyer, Abel, *The Political State of Great Britain*, 60 vols, 1711–40.

Broglie, J. V. A., duc de, *Histoire de la Politique étrangère de Louis XV*, 10 vols, Paris 1883–95.

Brooke, John, *George III*, 1974.

Brosses, Charles de, *L'Italie il y a cent ans, ou Lettres écrites d'Italie à quelques amis en 1739 et 1740*, ed. M. R. Columb, 2 vols, Paris 1836.

Browne, James, *A History of the Highlands and of the Highlands Clans*, 4 vols, Glasgow 1832–3.

Browning, Andrew, *Thomas Osborne, Earl of Danby and Duke of Leeds*, 3 vols, Glasgow 1944–51.

Broxap, Henry, *The Later Non-Jurors*, Cambridge 1924.

Burke, John, *A History of the Commoners of Great Britain and Ireland*, 4 vols, 1833–8.

Carson, Edward, *The Ancient and Rightful Customs*, 1972.

Charnock, John, *Biographia Navalis*, 6 vols, 1794–8.

Chesterfield, Philip D. Stanhope, 4th Earl of, *Letters of Lord Chesterfield*, ed. B. Dobrée, 6 vols, 1932.

Clark, J. C. D. 'The decline of party, 1740–1760', *English Historical Review*, xciii (1978) pp. 499–527.

Cobbett, William, *The Parliamentary History of England*, 36 vols, 1806–1820.

Cokayne, G. E., *Complete Baronetage*, 6 vols, 1900–1909, *Complete Peerage*, 14 vols, 1910–59.

Colin, J. L. A., *Louis XV et les Jacobites, le projet du débarquement en Angleterre de 1743-1744*, Paris 1901.

Colley, Linda, 'The Loyal Brotherhood and the Cocoa Tree: The London Organization of the Tory party 1727–1760', *The Historical Journal* xx (1977), pp. 77–95.

Collier, Cedric, 'Yorkshire and the Forty-Five', *The Yorkshire Archaeological Journal*, xxxviii (1952–5), pp. 71–95.

Journals of the House of Commons, 1803 ed.

Conduct of, *The Conduct of the late and present ministry compared; with an impartial review of public transactions since the resignation of the Right Honourable the Earl of Orford, and the causes that immediately effected the same*, 1742.

Cox, Marjorie, 'Sir Roger Bradshaigh, 3rd Bart., and the electoral management of Wigan', *Bulletin of John Rylands Library*, xxxvii (1954–5), pp. 120–64.

Coxe, William, *Memoirs of the life and administration of Sir Robert Walpole, Earl of Orford*, 3 vols, 1798.

Memoirs of Horatio, Lord Walpole, 2 vols, 1820.

Memoirs of the administration of the Rt. Hon. Henry Pelham, 2 vols, 1829.

Cruickshanks, Eveline, '101, Secret Agent', *History Today*, April 1969, pp. 273–6.

'The Tories and the succession to the Crown in the 1714 Parliament', *Bulletin of the Institute of Historical Research*, xlvi (1973), pp. 176–85.

Daiches, David, *Charles Edward Stuart*, 1975.

Dalton, Charles, *English Army Lists and Commissions Registers 1661–1714*, 6 vols, 1892–1904.

Dean, C. G. T., *The Royal Hospital, Chelsea*, 1950.

Dickinson, H. T., *Bolingbroke*, 1970.

Elcho, Lord, *Short Account of the Affairs of Scotland in 1744, 1745, & 1746*, Edinburgh 1973.

Ellis, K., *The Post Office in the Eighteenth Century*, 1958.

Erskine-Hill, Howard, *The Social Milieu of Alexander Pope*, 1975.

Ewald, Alexander Charles, *The Life and Times of Prince Charles Stuart*, 2 vols, 1875.

Fitzmaurice, Lord, *Life of William, Earl of Shelburne*, 2 vols, 1912.

Frederick II, *Oeuvres complètes*, 17 vols, Berlin 1790.

Foord, Archibald S., *His Majesty's Opposition 1714–1830*, Oxford 1964.

Fritz, Paul S., *The English Ministers and Jacobitism between the Rebellions of 1715 and 1745*, Toronto 1975.

Gentleman's Magazine, *The Gentleman's Magazine and Historical Chronicle*, 1730–51.

Gibbon, Edward, *Memoirs of my own Life*, ed. G. A. Bonnard, 1966.

Godley, A. D., *Oxford in the Eighteenth Century*, 1908.

Goldie, Mark, 'Edmund Bohun and *Jus Gentium* in the Revolution Debate 1689–93', *The Historical Journal*, xx (1977), pp. 569–86.

Gyllenborg, *Letters which passed between Count Gyllenborg, the Barons Görtz, Sparre and others*, 1717.

Haile, Martin, *James Francis Edward, the Old Chevalier*, 1917.

Hasted, Edward, *The history and topographical survey of the county of Kent*, 4 vols, Canterbury 1778–99.

Hay, D., Linebaugh, P. and Thompson, E.P., eds., *Albion's Fatal Tree*, 1977.

Hervey, John, Lord, *Some Materials towards Memoirs of the Reign of George II*, ed. Romney Sedgwick, 3 vols, 1931.

Hill, B. W., *The Growth of Parliamentary Parties 1689–1742*, 1976.

Historical Manuscripts Commission
  First Report (Richmond mss.), 1870.
  Tenth Report, Appendix iv (Bagot mss.), 1885.
  Twelfth Report, Appendix ix (Beaufort mss.), 1891.
  Fourteenth Report, Appendix ix (Trevor mss.), 1895.
  Fifteenth Report, Appendix vii (Puleston mss.), 1898.
  Fifty-sixth Report, Stuart Papers i, 1902, vi, 1916.
  Sixty-third Report, Diary of Viscount Percival, afterwards 1st Earl of Egmont 1730–47, 1920–3.
  Sixty-seventh Report, Polwarth mss. v, 1961.

Holmes, Geoffrey, *British Politics in the Age of Anne*, 1967.
  The Trial of Doctor Sacheverell, 1973.
Horley, Rev. E., *Sefton*, 1893.
Horwitz, Henry, *Parliament, Policy and Politics in the reign of William III*, Manchester 1977.
Houblon, Alice, Lady, *The Houblon Family*, 1907.
Howard, Joseph J., *Visitation of England and Wales*, 32 vols, 1893–1921.
Howell, T. B., *A Complete Collection of State Trials*, 34 vols, 1816–28.
Hunt, N. C., *Two Early Political Associations, the Quakers and the Dissenting Deputies in the Age of Sir Robert Walpole*, Oxford 1961.
Ilchester, Lord, *Henry Fox, First Lord Holland*, 2 vols, 1920.
Jarvis, Rupert C., *Collected Papers on the Jacobite Risings*, Manchester 1972.
Johnstone, Chevalier de, *A Memoir of the Forty-five*, 1820.
Jones, G. H., *The Main Stream of Jacobitism*, Harvard 1954.
Jones, J. R., *The Revolution of 1688 in England*, 1972.
Junius, *Letters of Junius*, 1791.
Kenyon, J. P., *Revolution Principles, the Politics of Party 1689–1720*, 1977.
Kettle, Anne J., 'The Lichfield Races', *Lichfield and S. Staffordshire Archaeological and Historic Society*, vi (1964–6), pp. 39–44.
King, William, *Political and Literary Anecdotes*, 1819.
Kirk, Rev. John, *Biographies of English Catholics in the Eighteenth Century*, 1909.
Lacour-Gayet, G., *La Marine militaire de la France sous le règne de Louis XV*, Paris 1910.
Lang, Andrew, *Pickle the Spy*, 1897.
Lipscomb, George, *The History and Antiquities of the County of Buckingham*, 4 vols, 1847–51.
Luynes, Philippe d'Albert, duc de, *Mémoires du duc de Luynes sur la cour de Louis XV*, ed. L. Dussieux et E. Soulié, 17 vols, Paris 1860–6.
Lodge, John, *The Peerage of Ireland*, revised by Mervyn Archdall, 7 vols, Dublin 1789.
Lyttelton, George, *Memoirs and Correspondence of George Lord Lyttelton*, ed. R. J. Phillimore, 1845.
  A Letter to the Tories, 1747 [by G. Lyttelton].
Mahon, Lord, *History of England from the Peace of Utrecht*, 7 vols, 1858.
  Letter to *The Times*, 29 Dec. 1864 [as Lord Stanhope].
Malmesbury, *A Series of Letters of the First Earl of Malmesbury, His Family and his Friends from 1748 to 1820*, 2 vols, 1870.
Manchester, Duke of, *Court and Society from Elizabeth to Anne*, 2 vols, 1864.

Manning, O. and Bray, W., *The History and Antiquities of the County of Surrey*, 4 vols, 1804–14.

Marion, M., *Histoire Financière de la France depuis 1715*, 6 vols, Paris 1927–31.

Marchmont, Earls of, *A Selection from the Papers of the Earls of Marchmont*, ed. Sir G. H. Rose, 3 vols, 1831.

Maxwell of Kirkconnel, James, *Narrative of Charles Prince of Wales's expedition to Scotland in the year 1745*, Edinburgh 1841.

Mitchell, A. A., 'London and the Forty Five', *History Today*, Nov. 1965, pp. 719–26.

Molineux, G., *Memoir of the Molineux Family*, 1882.

Morant, Philip, *The history and antiquities of the county of Essex*, 2 vols, 1768.

Mounsey, G. G., *Carlisle in 1745*, 1846.

Murray, John, *Memorials of John Murray of Broughton*, ed. R. F. Bell, (Scottish History Society, xxvii) Edinburgh 1898.

Namier, Sir Lewis, *The Structure of Politics at the Accession of George III*, rev. ed. 1957.
  Crossroads of Power, 1963.

Nash, T. R., *Collections for the history of Worcestershire*, 2 vols, Oxford 1894–5.

Newton, Lady, *The House of Lyme*, 1917.
  Lyme Letters 1660–1760, 1925.

Nichols, John, *The History and antiquities of the county of Leicester*, 4 vols, 1795–1815.

Nichols, John, *Literary Anecdotes of the Eighteenth Century*, 9 vols, 1812–1815.

Noailles, Adrien Maurice, duc de, *Mémoires politiques et militaires*, ed. Millot, 3 vols, Paris 1825.
  Correspondance de Louis XV et du maréchal de Noailles, ed. C. Rousset, 2 vols, Paris 1865.

Northumberland County History Committee, *A History of Northumberland*, 15 vols, 1893–1940.

Ormerod, George, *The History of the County Palatine of Chester*, 3 vols, 1882.

Orrery, Earls of, *The Orrery Papers*, ed. E. C. Boyle, Countess of Cork and Orrery, 2 vols, 1903.

Owen, John B., *The Rise of the Pelhams*, 1957.

Pauli, R., 'Actenstücke zur Thronbesteigung des Welfenhauses in England', *Zeitschrift des Historischer Vereins für Niedersachen*, Leipzig 1883.

[Perceval, Lord, by], *Faction Detected by the evidence of Facts:*

containing an impartial view of parties at home, and affairs abroad, 1742.

Piccioni, Camille, *Les Premiers Commis des Affaires étrangères au xviie et au xviiie siècles*, Paris 1928.

Quarterly Review, anon, 'William Borlase, St. Aubyn and Pope', cxxxix (1875), pp. 367–95.

Richelieu, L. F. A. du Plessis, duc de, *Mémoires authentiques du maréchal de Richelieu*, ed. A. de Boislisle, Paris 1918.

Richmond, H. W., *The Navy in the War of 1739–48*, 3 vols, Cambridge 1920.

Roberts, John Askew, *Wynnstay and the Wynns*, 1876.

Robinson, John, *The Delaval Papers*, Newcastle-upon-Tyne 1890.

Robson, R. J., *The Oxfordshire Election of 1754*, Oxford 1949.

Rogers, N., 'Popular disaffection in London during the Forty Five', *London Journal*, i 1–26.

'Popular Protest in early Hanoverian London', *Past and Present*, lxxix (1978), pp. 70–100.

Rudé, George, *Hanoverian London*, 1971.

Saint-Simon, Louis de Rouvroy, duc de, *Mémoires complètes*, ed. A. de Boilisle, 41 vols, Paris 1923–30.

Sautai, Maurice Théodore, *Les Préliminaries de la Guerre de la Succession d'Autriche*, Paris 1907.

Les Débuts de la Guerre de la Succession d'Autriche, Paris 1909.

Sedgwick, Romney, ed. *The History of Parliament; the House of Commons 1715–1754*, 2 vols, 1970.

Sharpe, R., *London and the Kingdom*, 3 vols, 1894–5.

Simpson, Llewellyn Eardley, *Derby and the Forty-five*, 1933.

Speck, W. A., *Tory & Whig. The Struggle in the Constituencies 1701–15*, 1970.

Tencin, Pierre et Alexandrine Guérin de, *Correspondance du cardinal de Tencin, ministre d'état et de madame de Tencin sa soeur avec la duc de Richelieu*, ed. B. de Laborde, Paris 1790 (in Bibliothèque Nationale).

Terry, Charles Sandford, ed., *The Forty-five. A narrative of the last Jacobite rising by several contemporary hands*, Cambridge 1922.

Thompson, E. P., *Whigs and Hunters. The Origin of the Black Act*, 1975.

Thomas, P. D. G., 'Jacobitism in Wales', *The Welsh History Review*, i (1962), pp. 279–300.

'Wynnstay versus Chirk Castle: Parliamentary elections in Denbighshire 1716–1741', *The National Library of Wales Journal*, xi (1959), pp. 105–23.

Twisden, Sir J. R., *The Family of Twysden and Twisden*, 1939.

Underdown, David, *Royalist Conspiracy in England 1649–1660*, New Haven 1960.

Vaucher, P., *Robert Walpole et la Politique de Fleury (1731–42)*, Paris 1924.

ed., *Recueil des Instructions données aux ambassadeurs et ministres de France, Angleterre 1698–1791*, Paris 1965.

Vaughan, H. M., 'Welsh Jacobitism', *The Transactions of the Honourable Society of Cymmrodorion*, 1920–1, pp. 11–39.

Vernon, Edward, *The Vernon Papers*, ed. B. M. Ranft, Navy Records Society, 1958.

Victoria History of the Counties of England, *A History of Warwickshire*, 9 vols, 1904–69.

Voltaire, *Précis du Siècle de Louis XV*, 2 vols, Paris 1826.

Oeuvres complètes, ed. Beuchot, 72 vols, Paris 1829–40.

Walpole, Horace, *Memoirs of the Reign of George II*, ed. Lord Holland, 3 vols, 1846.

Correspondence (Yale edition), ed. W. S. Lewis, 39 vols, New Haven 1937–74.

Waugh, W. T., *James Wolfe, Man and Soldier*, Montreal 1928.

Westminster Elections [A collection of broadsides relating to parliamentary elections 1741–51].

Yorke, Philip C., *The Life and Correspondence of Philip Yorke, Earl of Hardwicke*, 3 vols, Cambridge 1913.

Index